CAPE COD
Wampanoag
COOKBOOK

CAPE COD
Wampanoag
COOKBOOK

Wampanoag Indian Recipes, Images & Lore

10th of May 03

To Barbara —

*I love cookin smells;
they remind me of My Ancestors,
good times in Good eatin'!.
I have written with
Love
Earl Mills Sr*

Enjoy!

(Sachem & Troou Wampukak)

EARL MILLS SR.
Chief Flying Eagle, Mashpee Wampanoags
& BETTY BREEN

Clear Light Publishers
Santa Fe, New Mexico

Dedicated to Our Producers:
Emma Oakley Mills & Catherine McNiff Underhill
and to Mother Earth

ACKNOWLEDGMENTS

Each of us has a self-appointed guardian. Shelley Mills Pocknett and R. Paul Breen Jr., we appreciate the concern and support you have shown to your parents. Adrian Yelle and Ann Dittami Theroux, you are our mentors, our inspiration, and our idols. Special thanks to Bob Breen, Roger Burlingame, Kay and "Buzzy" Collins, Dr. Walton C. Galinat, Olin Kelley and Angus M. Miller Jr.; to our mascot, Miss Madas Pocknett; and especially to the Mills Family and the extended Breen Family. To the staff and clientele of The Flume restaurant, and to our many friends and relatives who contributed words of encouragement, recipes and blessings, thank you for making this book possible.

Clear Light Publishers
823 Don Diego, Santa Fe, New Mexico 87501
505-989-9590
www.clearlightbooks.com

First Edition
10 9 8 7 6 5 4 3 2

Library of Congress Cataloging-in-Publication Data
Mills, Earl.
    Cape Cod Wampanoag cookbook / Earl Mills Sr. & Betty Breen
      p. cm.
    ISBN 1-57416-057-5
      1. Indian cookery. 2. Indians of North America–Food. 3. Wampanoag
    Indians–Food. I. Breen, Betty. II. Title.
TX715 .M64995 2000
641.59'297–dc21

                             00-047544

Cover photograph © Mark Ferri, The Stock Market. Cover design by Marcia Keegan and Carol O'Shea. Interior design & typography by Carol O'Shea. Special thanks to Hobomock's Village at Plimoth Plantation, Plymouth, Massachusetts and the Mashantucket Pequot Museum and Research Center, Ledyard, Connecticut for use of photos in this book.

Printed in Canada.

CONTENTS

SEAFOOD

INTRODUCTION

Earl Mills Sr.

Feeding gruel to my ailing grandmother while I was still a very small child was the beginning of my long involvement with food, my elders and the rich heritage of my people. I quickly associated the loving relationship that resulted from that early experience with nourishment. Henceforth, food became synonymous with nurturing, nurturing with family, family with love, and love with my roots and the land.

My people have always lived by the seasons and relied on the gifts of the land and the sea for sustenance. We are attuned to the motions of the sun, the moon and the stars. We plant, harvest, hunt and fish according to nature's rhythm. Everything in life is related to an ever-growing circle with no beginning and no end, and that circle must be respected.

Generations, as well as seasons, overlap. My ancestors are with me as I prepare or enjoy favorite foods. I never make fish cakes and beans without feeling that my father is back in the kitchen with me. Potato Bargain always reminds me of my mother. My sister Delscena's spirit is beside me each time I fix up leftovers, because she could pull things out of any refrigerator and come up with a tasty meal.

From the time we were eight or nine years old, my brother Elwood and I led fishing and hunting expeditions. Like our father, grandfather and uncles before us, we prepared the boats, baited the hooks, rowed for the better part of a day and cleaned the fish for the men who hired us as Indian guides. Our father taught us how to fly cast as well as to use a rod and reel, the clamming rake and the eel spear. He taught us how to carry a gun safely and how to clean it. He taught us how to use an ax and a buck-saw and showed us the proper way to clean and cook game. He taught these skills exactly the way his own father had taught him.

Each fall we prepared and used snap scoops or rocker scoops to harvest cranberries, an enormous improvement over our ancestors' days on the bogs when they wrapped rags around their fingers for protection as they hand-picked the berries. The modernization of harvesting cranberries, like the evolution of corn, mirrors the history of my people as they have adapted to the changing landscape and population.

Cranberries, blueberries and strawberries were stored in our root cellar beneath shelves holding my mother's jams and jellies, mincemeat and pickles. Eggs in a solution called waterglass and salted, smoked or dried meats were also kept in the cellar. Living as close to the land as we did, we were well supplied with fresh food. We thought we were rich—we worked and played hard, and we lived and ate well.

Living in harmony with the land leads to a peaceful and grateful heart. My people give thanks whenever a fish, animal or vegetable is taken from Mother Earth. We offer a prayer to the spirit of the gift and promise that we won't take more than we need and that we will not waste anything we take.

Before opening my own restaurant in 1972, I worked at some wonderful old Cape Cod establishments in just about every capacity, learning the business from the cellar up. The more I learned at The Popponesset Inn, Wimpy's and the Coonamessett Inn, the more passionate I became about food, its preparation and presentation. All of my experience and all of my family traditions have contributed to my life's work and to this book.

My original intent for the *Cape Cod Wampanoag Cookbook* was to compile the many recipes I've carried in my head for a lifetime as well as those contributed by customers of my restaurant, The Flume. The dream only came to fruition when I met the ideal collaborator. Betty Breen interviewed me for a research paper she was assigned while in a graduate writing program. When I read her paper about a Thanksgiving meal shared by many cultures, I knew that I had found my writer.

In March of 1998 I handed Betty a brown paper bag stuffed with bits of paper. The recipe for my mother's favorite cake had been scribbled in pencil on the back of a student's hall pass back when I was Athletic Director of the Falmouth Schools. Another recipe was dated 1972. Some had been jotted down on sales slips or in margins of books. Three weeks later Betty presented me with an organized notebook containing over 100 edited recipes. We tested each, and soon a cookbook began to take shape.

To break up the cooking and eating, we took long walks. On these trips around the hidden paths of Cape Cod, I'd tell stories about the land and my people. On each ensuing visit, Betty would hand me several pages that I'd read in amazement. "How did you know this?" I'd ask. "You told me while we were walking," she said. I thought I was dealing with a psychic. She never took a note.

Betty is a writer who loves to cook, and I am a cook with stories to tell. Nothing in our backgrounds would have caused our paths to cross necessarily. We met over a research paper titled *A Common Table*.

So, join us in setting a common table with a focus on dishes that evoke happy memories. Grab your apron and follow me around the kitchen as we give thanks for the gifts of Mother Earth. And consider this Wampanoag philosophy:

Don't be timid about trying something new. No two-legged is perfect. Remember, **only** Kiehtan, the Principal Maker of All, is perfect.

The Flume restaurant, Mashpee, Massachusetts, on Cape Cod.

THE FIRST THANKSGIVING LIVES ON AT THE FLUME

Betty Breen

The Mashpee Wampanoag Indians celebrated the first Thanksgiving with the Plymouth colonists in 1621 (*see* story on p. 60). Spending Thanksgiving at the Cape, which my family loves to do, never seemed more appropriate than when I was working on this book with Earl Mills Sr., who is chief of the Mashpee Wampanoags. I arrived on the Cape several days ahead of my guests to get the house ready, bake pies and savor both the temporary solitude and the anticipation of the upcoming gathering. This would also be my chance to get photos of Earl's bustling kitchen at The Flume before the restaurant closed for the season.

Taking a break from my own preparations, I drove over to The Flume. The kitchen was a hive of activity, and pride in the pies I had left cooling on my own counter dissipated when I witnessed the work involved in cooking a total of over 200 pounds of turkey.

Bubbling on the back burners in the industrial kitchen were two enormous pots of turkey stock, one about 28 inches in height, the other slightly smaller, sending exotic aromas throughout the restaurant. The secret to the next day's rich gravy simmered in that stock. On a nearby chopping block lay veritable mountains of chopped onion and celery waiting to be sautéed and added to the neatly prepared bread cubes and spices; the stuffing was sure to be as scrumptious as the rest of the meal. Only the incessant ringing of the phone distracted "Aunt Jan" from chopping three cases of squash into symmetrical pieces.

"Will someone get the phone?" she begged.

"Hello, The Flume…," I said, obeying.

A very weak voice struggled with a painful and lonely request. Could someone from The Flume please deliver Thanksgiving dinner to two convalescent women, the caller asked.

My eyes darted to the wall where scraps of paper were haphazardly taped; these last-minute reservations that didn't fit into the overflowing reservation book would terrorize most kitchens. Lists of already-ordered outgoing dinners hung near the door. Earl didn't know yet about the last two calls, let alone this one.

But the excitement of the season overcame anxiety. Within minutes, Earl had taken six more turkeys out of the oven and changed out of his cooking clothes. Instead of taking pictures, I drove him to the home of that last caller to inform her that, of course, someone would deliver Thanksgiving dinner.

At the front door we were greeted by a suspicious, but soon-to-be-amused, shut-in who told us that she and her daughter were both sick. She was sad that she was going to miss both the holiday and her upcoming birthday. When we left, she was standing a little taller and still laughing about the owner of The Flume singing "Happy Birthday" on her doorstep and promising to deliver Thanksgiving dinner with all the fixings. The concern and generosity Earl expressed for this complete stranger showed the true spirit of Thanksgiving.

I reflected on the early settlers who helped themselves to the "goodly ears" of corn buried in small mounds at the mouth of the Pamet River and gave thanks for "God's good providence" while enjoying these fruits of Indian labor. Friendly and generous by nature, the Wampanoag people welcomed the first settlers to the shore only to discover that their innate sensibilities would eventually lead to change and loss. Some of Earl's people avoid the holiday; others demonstrate for a cause dear to their hearts. Earl remembers the original meaning of sharing the harvest's bounty, and The Flume prepares for a busy weekend.

This incident made me pause to reconsider the holiday season. Previously, I've wished that Thanksgiving could be moved to some obscure date in March so it wouldn't interfere with Christmas. Now I realize that the very juxtaposition of these festive occasions is rife with meaning.

Before the season of giving, a reminder to be thankful is fitting. The inspiring example of Earl's ancestors prompts us to share with those who suffer want or need, to celebrate other people's origins and to remember how we all got to this Common Table.

THE LEGEND OF WEETUCKS

Weetucks was the son of an aged squaw in a village of the Wampanoags, the People of the Light. When he was a very young boy, he disappeared from the tribe. Nothing was seen or heard from him for a full moon, about a month. One day he reappeared, falling exhausted on the path where the villagers would travel to get water. Kind hands carried him back to his mother's hut and laid him upon a bed of skins. For many days he tossed and turned and was delirious.

While he was recovering, he summoned the leading men of the tribe and instructed them in the use of roots, herbs, flowers, bark, berries and many other things. Some of this wisdom became well known, but other secrets of the boy named Weetucks have been closely guarded and remain sacred to the medicine men of the tribe.

Weetucks also taught the Wampanoags to make the shining fire. He taught the young boys to prepare for manhood and the young girls to prepare for womanhood. He taught the Wampanoags to be kind to strangers. To this day, our people are very kind to strangers.

Weetucks initiated his people into the sweat and mud bath ceremonies and taught them how to make pictures, to make wampum and to fashion canoes, spears, bows, arrows, shields and many implements useful in daily life. He was believed to be the son of Kiehtan.

After his recovery Weetucks went off to the woodlands to hunt. Upon his return home, he saw two strange figures huddled beside the fire inside the wetu, the round dwelling he shared with his mother. He offered to share the household food. But, when everything was put before them, the strangers snatched at the choicest portions and slunk back into the shadows. Weetucks and his mother spoke not a word.

Weetucks lay down but had trouble sleeping. Suddenly, a cold hand wakened him. Looking up, he saw the strangers' eyes gazing at him like four balls of fire. The two strangers said that they were the spirits of the departed and that they were sent by his father Kiehtan to warn him that his mother was now in the spirit land from the Southwest. They tried to comfort him by saying that all the living will someday meet the departed in the western heavens. In the morning when Weetucks looked upon his mother, he knew that she had passed on. He buried her with a death ceremony. Stones were heaped on her burial place and Weetucks lit a spirit fire over her grave.

It is believed that Weetucks was sent by his father Kiehtan to help his mother pass from the world of the living to the spirit land, and that her passing brought about a peace between the Wampanoags and their former enemies the Narragansetts. The next summer, the Narragansetts, the Turkey People who lived to the west, came to visit the Wampanoags. They smoked the pipe together and the conclusion of the hostilities brought about great rejoicing. Feasting lasted through the night and into the next day. The full beauty of the summertime was realized with the help of Kiehtan.

After having been sent as an emisssary from Kiethan, his father, Weetucks had completed his teaching. He bid the Wampanoag people *Wunni Montabon,* Good Morning. In the dawn light he walked across the waves of Narragansett Bay towards the western heavens.

THE FIRST COURSE

The Start of a New Day

A good meal should begin with a promise. Like the break of a new day, sharing bread with loved ones is a link in a continuous circle of life, family and nature. Sunrise is the symbolic start of each new day, an especially significant time to the Wampanoag people, whose name means "people of the light or the east."

As often as possible, I begin the day with a tobacco burning. Just as a meal may start out with a prayer and progress towards a sweet conclusion, a tobacco burning is a ceremony done at sunrise to greet the morning sun and to connect us to the spiritual world and to our ancestors. Tobacco is a sacred plant used for healing and for ceremony.

The ground is blessed before the fire is started. The fire is powerful, like the sun, which is a visible symbol as well as our connection to Kietannit, the spirit of Kiehtan, and to antiquity. Its smoke is our messenger. As the smoke rises, it permeates the spirit world and carries messages to the spirits, who in turn deliver our prayers and praise to Yotannit, the god of fire, and ultimately to Kiehtan, the Principal Maker of All. Everything is done for the approval of the spirits and to acknowledge the ancestors and our eternal connection to them.

I salivate on the tobacco and throw it onto the fire, symbolically uniting myself with the fire, with the spirits and with my ancestors through the smoke. As I add more tobacco, I motion to the Mannits, or gods, of an infinite number of things for which we give thanks and praise, including the directions, the winds, the oceans, the rains, the four-leggers and the two-leggers. I wrap myself in smoke, cleansing my body, and motion to the spiritual world with my hands and eyes. The directions of the north, east, west, south, and southwest and the directions inside each of us are important.

Left: Madas Pocknett and Billy Red Dove Mills, Earl's granddaughters, at the Youth Pow Wow in Mashpee.

Each of the directions has its own spirit. The east is significant because this is where we are as well as who we are. The southwest is where all the good souls go when they pass on to the next world. The sun goes out of the way or is lost in the west; this spirit combines with north and south to create violent or peaceful weather, respectively. The south is warm with no rain and combines with west and east to create ideal weather or dry, hot weather, respectively. The north brings the time for conferring one's blessings and preparing for the ongoing life cycle. The warm rains and winds come east from the southwest and nurture our beans, squash and corn—the Three Sisters—the basics of our early existence. The most essential direction, of course, is the one inside each of us.

Remnants of ancient fires, shell heaps and stones testify to the actual sites where my ancestors lived. As Native people we still celebrate their culture and heritage with pride. We have always been here; we are connected to the land.

Harvest bounty.

Earl demonstrating some dance steps at the Falmouth Historical Society.

We return thanks to our Mother,
The Earth, that sustains us.
To the wind,
That, moving the air, has banished diseases.
To our grandfather,
That has protected his grandchildren
And has given to us the rain.
To the sun,
That has looked upon the earth with a beneficient eye.

Earl's nephew, Anawan Weeden. Photo taken at Hobomock's Village at Plimoth Plantation. Used with permission from Plimoth Plantation, Plymouth, Massachusetts.

CHOWDERS & SOUPS

I think that if you can learn to make soup, you can make anything. Soup is the very basis of cooking. It is a combination of many ingredients—seasonings, spices and herbs, meats or fish and vegetables—and your own hand. When we were growing up, chowder or soup combined with good homemade bread and a delicious dessert made a hearty dinner.

My ancestors valued the gifts of Mother Earth. Every part of the vegetable, fruit, fish, or animal was used. The cooking methods I learned at the knees of these wonderful cooks and leaders are with me today; my people are beside me in spirit, guiding my hand making sure that I waste nothing.

FLUME QUAHOG CHOWDER

18 medium quahogs (2 cups meat,
  2½ cups juice)
1 medium onion, coarsely ground
2 medium potatoes, diced
9 tablespoons margarine
¼ pound salt pork
  OR 1 additional tablespoon
  margarine
10 tablespoons flour (level spoons)

1½ teaspoons salt
1 teaspoon black pepper
cream, half 'n' half, or milk to taste

Substitutions for fresh quahogs and juice:
2 10-ounce cans whole clams
2 8-ounce jars clam juice

Shuck quahogs, saving juice as well as meat. Rinse meat in the juice to remove pieces of shell and grit. Set meat aside. Drain juice into saucepan, screening out particles of shell and grit. Grind or chop quahogs coarsely and add to juice.

Cut salt pork into small pieces and sauté. Remove excess fat. Add onion, ½ teaspoon of the salt and 1 tablespoon of the margarine to the rendered salt pork, and sauté until onions are soft and translucent. (If not using salt pork, sauté onions in an additional 1 tablespoon of margarine.) Set aside. In a separate pan cook diced potatoes until soft with the remaining 1 teaspoon of salt in enough boiling water to cover. Drain and set aside. Over low heat, mix flour and remaining 8 tablespoons of margarine to make a roux. Set aside next to cooking area.

Cook quahogs, juice and onion mixture over medium high heat, stirring often with a wire whisk and bringing the mixture to a good simmer. Add the roux, continuing to cook and stir until the mixture thickens and you determine that the roux has cooked. Add cooked potatoes and black pepper, using a rubber spatula to fold in the ingredients. You now have 1 quart of Flume Chowder base.

Slowly add cream, half 'n' half or milk to the base, until it reaches your taste and desired consistency.

Heat "chowda" to a gentle simmer and serve in heated bowls. Add a grind of black pepper at the table. Accompany with sweet pickles and oyster or common crackers.

Serves 6.

EMMA'S FISH CHOWDER DELUXE

The following chowder was a special treat. My mother, Emma, would select a haddock from the fish man when he came by in his pickup truck. He would ring a bell to announce himself, then he'd cut, clean and fillet the fish on his tailgate. The head, bones and tail of the fish were included in the price. These were saved for the *everyday* chowder (*See* next page.)

2 medium potatoes
⅛ pound butter (½ stick)
1 medium onion, finely chopped
1 pound haddock, boned, skin on

1 quart light cream
1 teaspoon salt
¼ teaspoon pepper

Peel and dice potatoes. Boil in salted water until done, strain and set aside. Melt butter in large sauce pan and add finely chopped onion. Sauté onion until soft and clear.

Add haddock, light cream and potatoes. Let mixture heat up to just below simmer for about five minutes until fish is done. Add salt and pepper to taste. (*Note:* Do not stir the chowder unnecessarily as the fish may get too broken up. You can always break the pieces up, but you can't put them back together.) Remove the skin before serving. Heat the cups or bowls with hot water before adding the chowder.

Serves 6.

Earl's nephew, Anawan Weeden. Photo taken at Hobomock's Village at Plimoth Plantation. Used with permission from Plimoth Plantation, Plymouth, Massachusetts.

EVERYDAY CHOWDER

Unless she was preparing the special chowder above, my mother made a basic, down-home version from the head, bones and tail of the haddock. She'd bring the bones to a rolling boil, turn the kettle down and simmer for 15-20 minutes. Then she'd strain the broth and, while it was still warm, remove the fish from the bones and set this aside.

She'd add onions, sautéed in salt pork, a thickening of flour and water, cooked potatoes, seasonings and the fish to the stock. Sometimes she'd add a garni (bundle) of pickling spices and a bay leaf wrapped in cheesecloth. Just before serving, she'd add milk (she preferred canned milk). We smelled that chowder keeping warm on the wood stove while we did our chores, and our mouths watered in anticipation of its rich, sensual pleasure.

STOCK FOR SOUP

If you keep containers of stock in the freezer, you'll always have the basics for soups, chowders, sauces and many quick meals. Make sure you label and date everything in your freezer and rotate all of the items.

Use chicken and turkey bones right away to make stock. Cover bones with water, add half an onion, one carrot and two or three celery stalks, bring to a boil and simmer for 30–45 minutes. Now you have a delicious stock. It doesn't take long to throw soup together; just add left-over meat and vegetables. You can also use stock for a sauce or gravy. Turkey doesn't require as much salt or pepper as chicken stock.

To thaw frozen stock, place on lower shelf in the refrigerator overnight, or, for immediate use, place in warm water or use a microwave.

CREAM OF BROCCOLI SOUP

My broccoli soup stock is made the way my mother and grandmother made it, without the use of a food processor or blender. It is composed of the ends of onions, celery and broccoli—parts that others may simply toss away. You may add canned broth or base. You may also puree or blend your soup if you prefer this more modern method.

1 medium head broccoli
6 cups stock or water
1 cup onion, chopped
1 cup celery, chopped
2 teaspoons salt

½ teaspoon pepper
8 tablespoons butter (one stick)
½ cup flour
12 ounces evaporated milk, milk or cream

Trim and peel broccoli, cutting ½ inch off the end, and saving ends, trimmings, peelings and leaves. Add these, with onion, celery, salt and pepper, to 4 cups of rapidly boiling stock or water in large saucepan. Cover and simmer for 15 minutes. Strain thoroughly. Discard cooked vegetables and set strained liquid (stock) aside.

Meanwhile, chop florets and tender stems of broccoli and blanch in the remaining 2 cups of stock or water, about 3-4 minutes. Bring strained stock to a simmer in a large saucepan. Mix flour and melted butter well then add to the stock. Return to a boil, continuing to stir until stock is thickened and the flour is cooked. Add the stems, florets and stock. Stir and add milk and salt and pepper to taste. Simmer and serve.

The previous recipe can be adapted for any cream soup. Asparagus, leeks and potatoes, or watercress can be substituted for the broccoli.

Serves 6.

CORN CHOWDER

See recipe on page 129.

GAZPACHO

For those of you who enjoy a cold soup, the following rich gazpacho is a beautiful melange of colors, seasonings and shapes. The difference between your creation and commercially prepared products is immediately pleasing to all the senses, being superior in taste and aroma—and the varying sizes and shapes of the vegetables add to eye appeal.

1 cup carrots
1 cup red onion
1½ cups celery, peeled
½ cup cucumber
1½ cups fresh tomato
1 cup green and yellow peppers,
    mixed and seeded
½ cup parsley, chopped
12 cups tomato juice*
1 cup seasoned chicken stock
2 tablespoons capers with juice
1 teaspoon wine vinegar
2 teaspoons Tabasco sauce, or to taste

2 teaspoons Worcestershire sauce
2 tablespoons olive oil
3 buds garlic, minced
2 teaspoons salt
1 teaspoon black pepper
1 envelope unflavored gelatin**
optional: 2 tablespoons sugar
    I prefer Sacramento tomato juice. If another brand is used, you will probably need to add sugar.
    **More unflavored gelatin may be added if you desire a thicker gazpacho.*

Julienne the carrots. Chop the red onion. Cut the celery on the diagonal. Remove the seeds from the cucumber, but leave some of the green rind on for color. Remove the seeds from the tomato. Dice the cucumber, tomato, and green and yellow peppers. Chop the parsley. Add all of the vegetables to the juice. Stir well. Add remaining ingredients except gelatin, adjusting to your own palate. Dissolve the gelatin according to the directions on the box and add last.

Chill for at least 6 hours before serving.

Serves 18.

— . — . — . — . — . — . — . — . — . — . —

The first time I traveled to Portugal and saw the beautiful countryside, I felt very much at home with the landscape and farms, with the farmers and the fishermen. Portuguese sailors had long since found the shores of Fall River, New Bedford and Provincetown, having traveled west on fishing and trading ships in the last century. These excellent seamen and proficient farmers found that the landscape and waters of Cape Cod suited their talents, and they settled in and around the area, providing produce and fish, influencing recipes and culture and coexisting harmoniously with my people. The following two recipes were inspired by this rich culture.

— . — . — . — . — . — . — . — . — . — . —

KALE SOUP

1 gallon stock* or water
3½ cups onions, diced
4 cups cabbage, diced
1½ pounds kale, fresh or frozen, shredded
1 15½-ounce can red kidney beans
2–3 medium potatoes, cut in bite-sized pieces

1½ pound linguica (Portuguese sausage, or any sausage) thinly sliced
2–3 bay leaves
I prefer to use turkey stock for this recipe.

Bring the stock to a simmer in a large saucepan. Add the onions and cabbage. Simmer for 15 minutes. Add kale. Bring to a simmer again and simmer for another 30 minutes. Add the beans. Bring to a simmer again. Add potatoes, linguica and bay leaves. Simmer until the potatoes are tender, about 30 minutes. Remove bay leaves before serving.

Serves 24.

PORTUGUESE SOUP

(from Flume patrons Ann and Bill McWilliams)

2 tablespoons olive oil
4 garlic cloves, minced
1 onion, minced
1 small green pepper, minced
32 ounces chicken broth
28 ounces stewed tomatoes

black pepper
basil
parsley
rosemary
1½ pounds white haddock or cod
1 pound sea scallops

In a large saucepan, sauté garlic, onion and green pepper in olive oil. Add chicken broth and tomatoes. Mix in pepper and seasonings to taste. Bring to a boil. Shut off burner then add fish and scallops. Cover and let sit for 20 minutes. The flavor improves as it sits.

Serves 12.

SPLIT PEA SOUP

If we were having ham for dinner, I knew that very soon we'd be having pea soup or some kind of bean soup. We were taught to take good care of our pigs, to feed the "dumb animals" before we ate, but we didn't see our pigs as pets—they were ham or bacon.

2½ quarts stock or water
1 ham bone, left over from a baked
  ham with some meat still on it
2 cups split peas
1½ cups onion, chopped
1 cup celery, chopped

2 teaspoons salt
½ teaspoon pepper
2 bay leaves
optional, but highly recommended:
  1 cup carrots, grated

Bring stock or water to a boil in a large saucepan. Add the ham bone and simmer for 15 minutes. Add split peas, onions and celery and simmer until the peas are soft. Turn off heat. Remove bone and meat. Cut up cooled meat and return it to the pan. Bring the pan back to a simmer, add bay leaves, salt and pepper to taste.

If using carrots, add now and simmer an additional 2-3 minutes. Serve with garlic or croutons.

Serves 8.

"TURTLE BEAN" OR BLACK BEAN SOUP

All Native Americans revere the land. We refer to it as the turtle's back or Turtle Island. Like the land itself, the turtle is an ancient and respected being. Perhaps that's why we call black beans "turtle beans."

3–5 quarts stock or water
2 cups black beans
1 ham bone with some meat
1½ cups onions, chopped
1 cup celery, chopped
2 bay leaves

2 teaspoons salt
½ teaspoon pepper
1 cup dry sherry
garnishes: lemon, red onion and
   hard boiled egg

Bring 3 quarts stock or water to a boil in a large saucepan. (An additional 1–2 cups of water or stock will be needed subsequently to maintain the desired consistency.) Add beans, ham bone, onion and celery and continue to simmer for 1½ to 2 hours, until beans are soft. Remove ham bone. Discard bone and meat. Pour contents of saucepan into a food mill, food processor or blender. Process until smooth.

Return soup to saucepan. Add bay leaves, salt and pepper. Bring to a simmer, adding the necessary amount of water or stock to reach desired thickness, mindful that the sherry will further thin the soup.

Sherry is added immediately before serving. Garnish with a thin slice of lemon, chopped red onion and chopped hard-boiled egg.

Serves 8.

Photo taken at Hobomock's Village at Plimoth Plantation.
Used with permission from Plimoth Plantation, Plymouth, Massachusetts.

BREADS

■ ▪ ■ ▪ ■ ▪ ■ ▪ ■ ▪ ■ ▪ ■ ▪ ■ ▪ ■

Once home only to native people, Cape Cod at the millennium is a growing microcosm representing all ages, nationalities and creeds. Ann Theroux, contributor of the first bread recipe (below), is one of our mentors. She and her husband, Al, retired to Cape Cod after all of their children were grown.

One dreary day, Ann concocted this bread, making use of what was on the shelf and cheering up the house with a wonderful aroma. Al loved it so much he encouraged her to enter a cooking contest sponsored by Boston talk show host Dave Maynard. Bean Pot Bread was the winner of the first round of the contest and went on to win the final round at Quincy Marketplace in Boston.

■ ▪ ■ ▪ ■ ▪ ■ ▪ ■ ▪ ■ ▪ ■ ▪ ■ ▪ ■

BEAN POT BREAD
(from Ann Theroux)

1 package yeast
4 Weetabix biscuits or 2 large
   Shredded Wheat biscuits
2 cups lukewarm water
1 10½-ounce can Campbell's Bean
   with Bacon Soup
4 teaspoons dark brown sugar
¼ cup dark molasses
2 teaspoons salt
2 tablespoons shortening
1 egg, beaten
6 cups flour
optional: crisp bacon crumbs

Preheat oven to 350°. Grease loaf pans (either two large or three small pans) preferably with bacon fat.

Soak yeast and cereal biscuits in lukewarm water for 5 minutes. Add soup and next five ingredients. Beat until blended, then add flour gradually. Knead until smooth and not sticky. Let rise for half an hour. Put into greased pans. Top with bacon crumbs if desired. Let rise to top of pans—about one hour. Bake for about 50 minutes. Slices beautifully when cool.

Serves 8.

Indian woman cooking. Photo taken at Hobomock's Village at Plimoth Plantation.
Used with permission from Plimoth Plantation, Plymouth, Massachusetts.

INDIAN FRY BREAD

from Sonya, Karen and Cheryl Abe, Tuba City, AZ

3 cups flour
1¼ teaspoons baking powder
1/2 teaspoon salt

1½ cups warm water
1 cup vegetable oil

Mix flour, baking powder and salt. Add warm water and knead until dough is soft but not sticky. Tear off a medium-size piece and shape into a ball. Pat the dough flat. Use a rolling pin to further flatten dough. Heat vegetable oil in a skillet to sizzling hot. Gently place the flattened dough into the hot oil. Remove bread when it is brown on both sides. Serve hot, plain or with powdered sugar.

Serves 8.

EMMA OAKLEY MILLS' FRY BREAD
"Morning Bread"

This is also known as fried bread. My grandfather, Irving Oakley, nick-named it "morning bread," because that's when he loved to eat it with molasses and cream. My grandmother Christine passed her expertise along to my mother, Emma. You should have seen my mother fry these little breads. The pan would be smoking, but they'd never burn. This is amazing when you think about how many things she had going at the same time.

1 cup flour
¼ tablespoon salt
2 teaspoons baking powder
½ cup milk*
2 tablespoons oil or bacon fat

Tip: A black spider (cast iron pan) or pancake griddle is best for frying.
    Amount of milk varies with different types of flour.

Mix dry ingredients with milk, a little at a time, adding just enough milk to form a soft consistency like that of bread dough. **Do not overmix.**

Heat black spider (cast iron pan). Add half of the oil. Scoop the dough with a serving spoon and push it off into the pan with your index finger. Don't scoop too much more than a level spoonful or it won't cook through. Continue filling pan until full. Turn heat down after filling.

When the edges brown and the bubbles in the bread break, turn them, and add the rest of the oil. The second side will take half as long as the first. Brown well.

Serve with butter, jam, maple syrup, gravy, honey, molasses or cream—or just as they are, as a nice complement to stews, soups or stewed beans.

Serves 4.

"Aunt Jan" Hendricks, The Flume's baker, rolling out pastry.

PIE CRUST

2½ cups flour
3 tablespoons sugar
10 tablespoons margarine
1 egg

¼ cup ice water
2 teaspoons white vinegar

Preheat oven to 325°.

Mix flour and sugar. Blend in margarine until mixture has the consistency of coarse meal. Beat together egg, water and white vinegar. Add to flour mixture, using fork. Add more water, if necessary. If too wet, use more flour when rolling out.

Turn dough onto a lightly floured board. Knead for one minute. Divide dough. Shape into two flat cakes. Refrigerate for 30 minutes.

If making pasties, use about ½ cup of the filling of your choice for each 6-inch pasty. Lay the rounds on the pastry board with half of the round over the rolling pin and put in the fillings, dampen the edges lightly and fold over in a semicircle.

Shape the pasty nicely and "crimp" the extreme edges between the fingers and thumb. Cut a slit in the center of the pasty. Bake at 325° for about 20 minutes.

Turn oven to 375° and bake for another 20 minutes or until crust is golden brown.

Makes two 6-inch pasties.

APPLE CHUNK BREAD

This is delicious to eat as well as fun to make, and it makes the whole house smell wonderful. It's even better the second day, if it lasts that long. I like to slather it with cream cheese.

2 cups apples, finely chopped
1 cup molasses
1 cup sugar
2 beaten eggs
1 cup melted butter
1 cup milk
4 cups sifted flour

1 teaspoon baking soda
1 teaspoon cinnamon
1 teaspoon cloves
1 teaspoon vanilla extract
1 teaspoon lemon extract
optional: 1 cup raisins and/or 1 cup chopped walnuts.

Preheat oven to 350°.

Grease and flour 1 tube pan or 2 loaf pans (8 x 4 x 4 inches). Recipe can be halved for one loaf pan.

Combine the finely chopped apples with the cup of molasses in a medium saucepan. Boil 5 minutes. Cool slightly.

Mix remaining ingredients well. Stir in the apples and molasses. Bake 1 hour for tube pan, about 45–50 minutes for loaf pans.

Serves 12–14.

BAKING POWDER BISCUITS

See recipe on page 169.

BANANA NUT BREAD

2 cups all-purpose flour
1½ teaspoons baking soda
½ teaspoon salt
¾ cup sugar
8 tablespoons butter, melted (1 stick)

2 eggs
1½ cups mashed bananas
¾ cup chopped walnuts or pecans
2 teaspoons lemon rind
2 tablespoons sugar

Preheat oven to 350°.

Grease a loaf pan (8 x 4 x 4 inches). Whisk together the flour, baking soda and salt. In a separate bowl, cream the butter and and the first ¾ cup of sugar with the eggs for 2 minutes. Add the mashed banana and mix for an additional 30 seconds. **Do not overmix.** Fold in the flour mixture and add the nuts. Mix the lemon rind with the additional 2 tablespoons of sugar and sprinkle over the batter.

Bake for 50–60 minutes.

Serves 8.

CORN BREAD

See recipes on pages 130, 132, and 133.

CRANBERRY BREAD

See recipes on pages 148 and 150.

IRISH SODA BREAD
(from Ellen "Elsie" Nagel Roche)

2 cups milk
2 tablespoons vinegar
4 cups flour
1 teaspoon salt
½ cup sugar
2 teaspoons baking soda
1 tablespoon caraway seeds

½ box raisins
1 egg, fork beaten
1 stick butter, melted

Optional glaze:
2 teaspoons butter, slightly softened
1 tablespoon confectioner's sugar

Preheat oven to 350°. Lightly grease and flour pans—either one tube pan or 2 loaf pans (9 x 4 x 4 inches).

Add vinegar to milk. Set aside to sour and thicken. Sift together flour, salt, sugar and baking soda. Toss caraway seeds and raisins with dry ingredients. Add melted butter, soured milk and beaten egg and mix well.

Bake for 40–45 minutes. Glaze can be prepared after bread is removed from oven. Spread butter on crust while bread is still hot. Sift sugar over bread.

Serves 16.

JALAPEÑO & CHEDDAR CORN BREAD

See recipe on page 134.

LEMON BREAD

⅓ cup butter
2 eggs
grated rind of one lemon
1 teaspoon baking powder
1 cup white sugar
½ cup milk
1½ cups flour

Topping:
juice of one lemon
½ cup white sugar

Preheat oven to 350°. Lightly grease and flour one 8 x 4 x 4-inch loaf pan.

Combine all ingredients except those for the topping. Blend thoroughly (the more you beat it, the better it will be). Bake for 1 hour.

While bread is baking, prepare topping. Mix the juice of one lemon with ½ cup of sugar and let stand. Stir mixture and pour over bread when you take it out of the pan.

Serves 8–10.

ZUCCHINI BREAD

4 eggs
2 cups sugar
1 cup vegetable oil
1½ teaspoons vanilla
3½ cups flour
1 teaspoon salt

1½ teaspoons baking soda
¾ teaspoon baking powder
1 teaspoon cinnamon
2 cups grated zucchini
1 cup chopped nuts
1 cup raisins

Preheat oven to 350°. Grease and flour two loaf pans (8 x 4 x 4 inches).

Beat eggs and sugar until frothy. Add oil and vanilla. Sift dry ingredients together and add to egg mixture. Combine remaining ingredients and fold in.

Bake for 1 hour.

Serves 14–16.

SALADS & DRESSINGS

CAESAR SALAD

2 garlic cloves, peeled
8 croutons
8 anchovy fillets
1 egg
juice of 1 lemon
½ teaspoon dry mustard
1 tablespoon Worcestershire sauce

1 tablespoon wine vinegar
4 tablespoons olive oil
3 drops Tabasco sauce
4 tablespoons Parmesan cheese
1 head romaine lettuce
1 teaspoon black pepper
salt to taste

Place garlic into a very dry wooden bowl and smash with a fork. Sprinkle lightly with salt and press mashed garlic into the bowl with a serving spoon. Wipe the bowl with a few croutons to pick up some of the garlic. Set croutons aside.

Mince and add 6 of the anchovies. Whip and add an egg. Squeeze the lemon through cheesecloth or use another careful method to prevent seeds from becoming part of the dressing. Add the lemon juice, dry mustard, Worcestershire sauce, vinegar, oil and Tabasco sauce.

Sprinkle 3 tablespoons of the Parmesan cheese on the surface of dressing and whip with a fork until smooth. Add the greens and toss. Add black pepper and toss again.

Sprinkle remaining cheese and remaining 2 anchovies on top.

Serves 6.

THE FLUME COLE SLAW

6 cups cabbage, shredded
¼ cup sugar (scant measure)
¼ cup cider vinegar (generous measure)
1 pint mayonnaise
2 tablespoons celery seed*

optional: green pepper, minced; carrots, shredded; parsley, chopped; raisins, soaked
Use more or less celery seed as preferred.

Shred cabbage and cut in half if shreds are too long. Set aside. Put sugar in a bowl. Add vinegar and whip until sugar is dissolved. Add mayonnaise and thoroughly fold into the vinegar/sugar mixture. Spoon mixture over cabbage—amount of dressing will depend on your own personal preference. Add celery seed and remaining optional ingredients as desired.

If using raisins, soak first to soften.

Serves 6.

GRANDMOTHER'S SALAD
(from Thomas W. Hutchinson)

This salad is a very nice complement to a corn and fish dinner, or maybe with some fried squash.

1 large cucumber
2–3 large ripe tomatoes
juice of 1 lemon

½ cup sugar
salt and pepper to taste

Peel and slice cucumber fairly thick. Slice an equal amount of tomatoes, a bit thicker.

Mix the juice of one lemon and enough sugar to sweeten it. Add to the cucumber and tomatoes. Add salt and pepper to taste.

Chill several hours. Stir before serving.

Serves 6.

VINAIGRETTE DRESSING

1 garlic clove, minced
½ teaspoon tarragon
2 tablespoons red wine vinegar*
1 teaspoon salt
2 grinds, black pepper

1 teaspoon Dijon mustard
5 tablespoons olive oil
optional: basil, parsley
*4 teaspoons balsamic vinegar may be substituted for the red wine vinegar.

Mince garlic and tarragon together. Combine with vinegar, salt, pepper and mustard in a small bowl. Whisk in oil drop by drop until an emulsion is formed. Add the rest of the oil in a thin stream, whisking for 2–3 minutes. Add the basil and parsley.

Serves 4.

Variety of egg beaters that are family heirlooms are
used as decorations on the wall at The Flume.

SAUCES

These sauces may be used alone over pasta or combined with meat and/or vegetables in various ways. Additional sauce recipes can be found in the chapters on meats, seafood, and vegetables.

ALFREDO SAUCE
(for Fettuccine Alfredo)

¼ pound butter
¾ cup Parmesan cheese
½ cup light cream
1 egg, slightly beaten
salt

Fettuccine Alfredo
1 tablespoon olive oil
1 pound fettuccine
ground black pepper

Melt butter. Gradually add cheese, cream and beaten egg and blend until thickened.

For Fettuccine Alfredo: cook pasta in salted boiling water with olive oil. While pasta is cooking, make sauce. When pasta is done, toss with sauce. Add ground pepper to taste at the table.

Serves 4.

Warren "Woggie" Hicks making sauce in The Flume's kitchen.

ANCHOVY BUTTER

1 2-ounce can anchovy fillets,
saving the oil

2 tablespoons butter, margarine or
olive oil,
OR a combination

Place the anchovies, including the oil, in a sauté pan. Add the butter, or olive oil, or a combination of both. Heat to lukewarm and scramble with a fork or a whip. **Do not cook. This would toughen the anchovies.** The anchovies should just meld into the butter.

Stir thoroughly when serving. More butter may be added to taste. Serve on swordfish, halibut, scrod or salad.

Serves 6.

ANCHOVY SAUCE
(for pasta)

1 tablespoon olive oil
1–8 anchovies, to taste
1 cup broccoli, steamed & chopped

Pasta with Anchovy Sauce:
pasta of your choice
2 grinds fresh pepper
1 tablespoon Parmesan cheese

Prepare sauce while pasta is cooking. Heat oil in sauté pan. Add anchovies and mush. Add broccoli with some of its own water and sauté.

To serve with Pasta: Toss with cooked pasta. Add fresh pepper and Parmesan cheese. Toss again. Serve immediately.

Serves 2.

BARBECUE SAUCE

The following makes a great sauce for outdoor cooking just as it is, without processing.

6 cups tomatoes
1 cup brown sugar
¾ cup vinegar
1 lemon, juiced

2 medium onions, cut coarsely
¼ cup dry mustard
2 cups chili sauce
1½ teaspoons black pepper

Combine all ingredients. If not using right away as a sauce for outdoor cooking, simmer over low heat until the onions are soft. Pour the mixture through a food mill, if available. Otherwise, pour into a blender and blend until smooth. May be bottled for future use.

Optional: More flavor may be added if the sauce is cooked on racks of pork ribs.

CLAM SAUCE

See recipes for white and red versions on page 91.

CREAM SAUCE
Basic White Sauce

3 cups milk
6 tablespoons margarine
6 tablespoons flour
¾ teaspoon salt
¼ teaspoon white pepper

Supreme Sauce:
Add 1½ teaspoons chicken base

Scald the milk in a double boiler over high heat. Turn heat to medium high and keep milk warm.

In another pan, melt the margarine and add the flour, stirring continually until the consistency resembles corn meal. Add 2 cups of the scalded milk and heat the mixture to bubbling, continually whipping. Add the rest of the milk. Continue to whip, keeping mixture smooth and thick.

Add the salt and pepper sparingly. If using chicken base, add sparingly. Taste for flavor.

CREOLE SAUCE

½ cup onions, coarsely chopped
½ cup celery, coarsely chopped
1 tablespoon olive oil
1 14½-ounce can tomatoes
½ cup green bell pepper, coarsely
   chopped
1 bay leaf

salt and pepper to taste
¼ cup parsley, chopped
1 teaspoon cayenne or bay seasoning
2 tablespoons water
2 tablespoons cornstarch
6 medium white mushrooms, sliced
optional: 6–8 olives, sliced

Lightly sauté the onions and celery in the olive oil. Chop the tomatoes into small pieces. Add the peppers and the tomatoes to the pan and bring to a simmer. Add bay leaf, salt, pepper, parsley and cayenne or bay season-ing. Simmer the vegetables until peppers are tender.

   Combine water and cornstarch and add to the pan. Fold in the mush-rooms and remove the pan from the heat. If using olives, add with the mushrooms.

Serves 6–8.

EGG SAUCE

3 tablespoons margarine
2 tablespoons flour
1 cup warm milk
salt and pepper to taste

2 eggs, hard boiled and coarsely cut
1 tablespoon chopped parsley
optional: pinch of MSG (Accent)

Melt margarine over low heat. Add flour and blend. Cook until mixture begins to look like corn meal, then add warm milk, stirring constantly. Cook and stir with a wire whisk until sauce is thick and smooth.

   Add salt, pepper and eggs. Set aside in top of double boiler to keep warm. Add parsley just before serving.

Serves 4–6.

ITALIAN MEAT SAUCE
(Courtesy of George and Mary Diblasi)

Any recipe using uncooked meat on the bone needs to simmer for 3–4 hours to maximize the flavor from the bone. We let this sauce simmer for several hours and found it to be the best sauce we ever tasted!

2 tablespoons virgin olive oil
1 onion, chopped
4 cloves garlic, diced
5 cups water
3 28-ounce cans crushed tomatoes
¼ teaspoon–1 tablespoon black
  pepper
1 tablespoon salt
1 tablespoon basil
  OR 4 fresh basil leaves
1 tablespoon oregano
optional: ¼ teaspoon–1 tablespoon
  red pepper to taste.

Meats for Sauce
Meatballs:
1 pound hamburger meat
2 eggs
½ cup water
½ cup bread crumbs
¼ cup Parmesan cheese, grated
salt and pepper to taste
olive oil for cooking

1 pound Italian sausage, hot or
  sweet, or both
1 pound chunk of pork, bone in

Brown chopped onion and diced garlic in olive oil. Add water and all remaining sauce ingredients and simmer for at least one hour.

While sauce is simmering, prepare meatballs. In a large bowl, mix by hand hamburger meat, eggs, water, bread crumbs, Parmesan cheese, salt, and pepper, keeping hands moistened with water. Shape into meatballs the size of golf balls. Sauté in olive oil until slightly browned. Set aside.

Using the same oil, sauté the sausages and pork until browned on the outside. Meats shouldn't be cooked through at this time; they'll do so in the simmering sauce.

Add prepared meat to sauce and simmer for two more hours. The longer it cooks, the better it tastes.

Serves 24.

MARINARA SAUCE

3 cloves garlic
2 teaspoons basil*
1 tablespoon parsley*
4 tablespoons olive oil
6 ripe tomatoes, peeled and seeded
   OR 1 2½-pound can solid pack
   tomatoes

salt and pepper to taste
sugar to taste
   More basil and parsley may be used.

Sauté garlic, basil and parsley in olive oil. Add tomatoes and heat through.
Serves 2.

NEWBURG SAUCE

Delicious with scrod, a Flume favorite—see page 79.

1 pound lobster meat
2 tablespoons butter

½ cup dry sherry
3 cups Cream Sauce (*See* p. 26.)

Sauté lobster meat in the butter until the color begins to come off and
meat is coated. Add half the dry sherry and simmer for 10–15 seconds,
coating meat with the sherry. Add the necessary cream sauce to compliment the lobster meat. Bring to a simmer for 30 seconds. Add the remainder of the sherry to thin the sauce or add flavor if desired.

   Serve with toast points and a garnish of fresh pineapple. May also be
served with crab cakes, scrod or haddock.

Serves 4 as an entree or 6 as a sauce.

ORANGE SAUCE

See recipe in the Game chapter, on p. 41.

PASTA PRIMAVERA
(Clam Base, for Pasta Primavera)

Choose your favorites, enough for 2 servings. Suggestions include bok choy, mushrooms, broccoli, onions, julienned or thinly sliced carrots, summer squash, garlic, zucchini, and green onions.

1 tablespoon olive oil
½–1 cup clam broth, enough to coat veggies
2 grinds fresh black pepper
1 tablespoon Parmesan cheese

Chop the vegetables and sauté in oil. When almost done, add clam broth and pepper.

Toss with pasta and Parmesan cheese.

Serves 2.

Photo taken at Mashpee Pow Wow.

WELSH RAREBIT

1 quart milk
¼ pound margarine
½ cup flour
½ pound sharp white cheese, grated
½ pound sharp yellow cheese, grated
salt and pepper to taste
1 tablespoon dry mustard

flat beer or bourbon to taste
  (to thin)
2–5 tablespoons Worcestershire
  sauce
1 tablespoon horseradish
2–3 shakes curry powder
2 teaspoons Tabasco sauce

Heat the milk in a double boiler. In a separate, small pan, stirring constantly over low heat, make a roux with the margarine and flour. Add the roux to the heated milk, stirring constantly. Bring to the desired consistency then add the cheeses. (Cheese won't thin the sauce.) Whip the cheeses into the cream sauce with a wire whip.

Mix the dry mustard with a small amount of flat beer or bourbon. Combine with the Worcestershire sauce, horseradish, curry powder and Tabasco sauce, then add to cheese mixture, tasting for flavor. Add additional flat beer or bourbon as necessary to thin the sauce, especially for a later serving.

Serve over a broiled tomato (*See* p. 121.) or your favorite vegetable with a slice of bacon. Can also be served on crackers, dry bread or vegetables.

Serves 6–8.

MEATS

WINTER (Pap-on-a-kees-a-wush, The Time of the Long Moon)

We began planning for the cold season long before it arrived. My father, Ferdinand Mills, was persnickety about the fall harvest. He had his own way of digging and storing potatoes. The pole beans would be tied together with the squash and corn to unite the Three Sisters. Most onions, carrots and beets were kept in the salt hay and soil in the cellar, but some were left in the ground under salt hay to sweeten with the first frost.

Meantime, because of the colder weather, we'd probably be getting ready to slaughter a pig. Now, if a pig were hung in the garage, it wouldn't spoil before it got smoked or salted or whatever. To fatten up the pigs, we weaned them off the garbage and fed them cooked or scalded grains and corn.

I remember my first experience with slaughtering a pig. I was a pre-teen. Several of us converged on Mr. Bernard Carter's home. He lived diagonally down the street from us, where he had a little variety store, gas station and ice delivery business. He also raised a few pigs.

That year he was tired of the pigs and planned to get rid of the sow and the big boar. The Giffords from Marstons Mills were going to do the slaughtering, because they had the proper equipment. The boar was so big it was hard to get a hold of him. He was so big and strong and ornery that Mr. Carter told me to go up to the house and get my father's 410 and a couple of slugs. "We gotta take care of this pig," he said. "Then we'll stick him and save the blood for pudding."

So I got the gun and came back. Mr. Carter said, "Set it up." I was surprised that he was going to let me do the shooting. Prior to that time, I had only shot a few rabbits. So I loaded the gun and set it up on top of the fence, and the boar came on my side of the fence and began to make snorting and grunting sounds. Mr. Carter said, "When he turns and looks at you, try to get him between the eyes if you can, just up above and between the ears and the eyes."

Photo by Aaron Gooday taken at the Mashantucket Pequot Museum and Research Center, Ledyard, Connecticut. Used with permission.

I'm not sure that I could do that today, but that was how we lived then, and I didn't have any qualms about it. Matter of fact, I felt like an adult. When that pig looked at me, I pulled the trigger. I could see the bullet hit square between those ears and those eyes. That pig went down, and the men jumped on him and stuck him and saved the blood. They took the pig to the slaughterhouse and returned him to my father. The pig was quartered so my father could easily handle it for smoking, pickling, and corning.

Eating and making money went hand in hand. We made use of everything and wasted nothing. All parts of an animal or fish were useful. We always made use of every part of the pig, saving the lungs, liver, kidneys, and some of the intestines for sausages. Sometimes the men would float the intestines in the river to cleanse them for use as sausage casings. Head cheese was made from the head. More of a luncheon meat with a gelatinous broth than a cheese, head cheese was cooked for a long time with salt, pepper, onions, bay leaves and poultry seasoning—maybe a little hot sauce or hot pepper for a little zip, then cooked down until it became jellied. My dad loved a head cheese sandwich with horseradish sauce made from the horseradish in the backyard. I'd never try it when I was a kid, but in later years, I just loved it myself.

My mother made a delicious "light" stew with white dumplings, a lot of gravy, potatoes, carrots and parsnips from my dad's garden. I never asked what the "lights" were—it was just so good. I found out later that the lights were the lungs of the pig. That didn't change anything; the stew was still delicious.

We didn't pickle the pig's feet, but we used them in soups like pea soup.

My father smoked the pig. He'd also make linguica, chourica and sausage—grinding the meat up and stuffing it with a funnel into the well-washed intestine casings. Those were the days.

Coon hunting and rabbit hunting were part of life, too. My Uncle George and his group would come home with 45–50 rabbits. There was no way to freeze them in those days, so they salted and hung them up. Winters were always much colder then, so the rabbits would keep, hung outside on the barn or in the garage so the dogs couldn't get to them. Also, by December, there'd be raccoon skins hanging and drying on the garage.

In January and February we'd get out the rods and reels, in preparation for the fishing season ahead. We oiled the reels, repaired the eyes on the rods, took care of the handles, and checked the fishhooks and flies for fly fishing. Every year our boats would be scraped, caulked and painted inside and out. I adopted one of the boats as my own and painted

Uncle George "Two Deer" Oakley with wife, Alice Webquish, c. 1929.

"Smutt" on both sides of the bow. That was my father's nickname, and I thought it should also be mine. My father and my brother Elwood were great fly fishermen.

My brother and I became Indian guides just like my father and grandfather. Getting ready for the long days on the water contributed to our passion for hunting and fishing.

GIFTS OF THE SACRED WOODLANDS

My father, Ferdinand Mills, was the caretaker of a sportsman's lodge called Tanampo, which meant gun or rifle club. He also served as a guide for the men who came great distances to hunt and fish. Eating, drinking and sharing stories about the woodlands and waters were as much a part of the camaraderie as was the gunning.

One of the men inadvertently provided a story of his own. Eben Queppish was an excellent hunter as well as the camp cook. He cooked whatever was on hand. One time the hunters returned with nothing. Queppish was caught short and had to go out at the last minute to see what he could find for the hunters' dinner.

Shortly before dinner, my father's curiosity was aroused. The aromas coming from the stove were unfamiliar and unappetizing. Later, when he tried to cut the meat he had been served, the knife bounced right back off like it was a rubber chicken. Eben admitted that the only thing he had found was a blue heron.

Ferdinand, a fussy eater, complained, "That old bird was so tough you couldn't even cut the gravy."

From that time, this story ranked right up there with the many tales of hunting and fishing told by the camp cooks, hunters, fishermen, guides and caretakers!

Photo by Aaron Gooday taken at the Mashantucket Pequot Museum and
Research Center, Ledyard, Connecticut. Used with permission.

I raise my heart in thanks
To the Creator of the Sacred Woodlands
For the bounty.
Thanks to our Mother, the Earth,
Who sustains and nurtures us.
And to the family of Spirits
Who guide and oversee us
In our communication
With the Great Mystery.

GAME

ROAST (FARM) DUCK
Duck Stock & Gravy

Although farm ducks are domestic birds, we decided to include this delicious recipe here, so all the duck recipes are together for the reader's convenience.

3 ducks
½ medium onion, sliced
2 stalks celery, chopped
1 teaspoon salt
½ teaspoon black pepper
1–2 cups chicken or duck stock or water

cornstarch or arrowroot for thickening
optional: ½ medium apple, chicken base

Stuffing of your choice, if desired

Preheat the oven to 400°.

Remove the giblets from the ducks. Cut off and dispose of the excess neck skin and some of the excess fat. Place giblets and neck on a wire rack. Wash the duck thoroughly inside and out under cold water. Place on top of the giblets and neck on the rack. Add onions, celery, apple (if using), salt and pepper to the cavities.

Place the the rack in a roasting pan and the pan in the middle of the hot oven. Drain the fat after 45 minutes and every 15 minutes thereafter. Cook for a total of two hours.

Remove the ducks from the roasting pan. Place 2–4 cups of water or stock in the roasting pan and place on a burner. (Stock will make the duck sauce richer. This is a good time to make use of your frozen chicken or turkey stock.) If making orange sauce (*see* recipe on page 41), save some duck stock.

Before removing the wire rack from the pan, scrape off all pieces of meat. Cook the neck, giblets and essence, continually scraping the bottom of the pan. Add salt and pepper to taste. If using chicken base, adjust salt.

Strain the stock and save the giblets. If the giblets are still soft enough to cut, add them to the stock after thickening for a natural gravy. Thicken the stock over a medium heat with a mixture of water and cornstarch or arrowroot until result is just thick enough to coat a spoon or ladle.

When serving, cut the duck in half lengthwise and debone except for the wing and leg. If desired, stuff with Turkey Stuffing (*see* recipe on p. 62) substituting duck stock and giblets. You may add some applesauce to the stuffing to make an apple dressing.

Serves 6.

GAME BIRDS

Rinse game birds clean in salt water and let stand until they reach room temperature before roasting. The Salmi Sauce (*see* below) is used to marinate and tenderize wild duck and goose and reduce their gaminess as they cook.

SALMI SAUCE
(for wild duck or goose)

2 tablespoons butter	3 tablespoons cornstarch
½ cup onion	2 tablespoons duck stock*
½ cup celery	salt and pepper to taste
½ cup red wine	additional butter for topping
1 cup duck stock*	**If duck stock is unavailable, chicken*
2 teaspoons lemon juice	*broth may be substituted*

Prepare the duck or goose as directed below. Thinly slice the onion and celery and sauté in 2 tablespoons of butter. Add the ½ cup of red wine and simmer for 15 minutes to reduce.

After removing the duck or goose from the pan, return the pan to the heat on top of the stove, adding enough stock or broth to bring the liquid in the pan to a cup plus. Add the celery mixture and lemon juice to the pan and simmer while deglossing the bottom of the pan. Strain the mixture.

Just before serving, thicken sauce with a mixture of cornstarch and stock, adjusting taste with salt and pepper as desired. Add a few dabs of butter to the top of the bird.

WILD DUCK

Preheat oven to 350°.

Stuff duck cavity with sliced apples and celery tops. Place strips of bacon over the breast and add 1½ cups of water or chicken stock, along with the neck and giblets, to the pan.

For a well-done duck, roast 15 minutes per pound, basting every 15 minutes with the fat and stock in the pan, along with a mixture of 2 tablespoons of butter and ½ cup of red wine.

GOOSE

Preheat oven to 350°.

Do not stuff. Place celery leaves and sliced onion inside the cavity. Place strips of bacon over the breast.

Add 1½ cups of water or chicken stock to the pan along with the neck and giblets. Baste with pan drippings and 2 tablespoons of butter and ½ cup red wine. Roast at least 2½ to 3 hours or until done.

Serves 6.

PHEASANT

Preheat oven to 350°.

Place strips of bacon over the breast. Add 1 cup chicken stock to roasting pan and baste with drippings and a mixture of 2 tablespoons of butter and ½ cup red wine. Roast at least 30–45 minutes or until done.

Serves 4.

GROUSE, QUAIL, PARTRIDGE, PLOVER OR WOODCOCK

Preheat oven to 350°.

Brush with melted butter. Baste 3 more times with melted butter during baking. Add ½ cup water or stock to the bottom of the pan. Roast until tender, approximately 20–30 minutes.

When done, cut at joints into serving size pieces.

ORANGE SAUCE
(for Duck)

peel and skin of 1 orange
2 cups orange juice
2 tablespoons vinegar
3 tablespoons sugar
1–2 cups duck stock, seasoned

4 tablespoons corn starch
2 tablespoons brandy
3 tablespoons orange Curaçao
water to thin the cornstarch

Peel an orange and julienne the skin. Simmer in water to soften the peel and remove its bitterness.

Cook orange juice, vinegar and sugar until reduced to a syrup. Add the duck stock and bring to a simmer. Thicken with a mixture of cornstarch and water—just thick enough to coat a spoon or a ladle. Add the brandy and orange Curaçao and cook for 2–3 minutes. Add the blanched orange peel.

Serves 6.

Entrance to The Flume.

Betty's Thoughts on Game Hunting

Earl taught me many lessons in his outdoor classroom while we were preparing this book together. One crisp wintry afternoon we walked past Webster's Springs and along the Mashpee River where generations of his people hunted at Quinaquissett, "the Place of the Winding Path." Below us, the ocean trickled in, mingling with the fresh river water and gradually transforming riverbanks until they were awash with swaying sea grass. As we approached clumps of trees, great blue herons took flight, casting shadows with their enormous wings. Some thirty feet below our path, one gray and four snowy swans nonchalantly scoured the shallow waters for sustenance.

Earl recalled earlier days when the hunters gathered at his home early in the morning. His mother would have their favorite foods ready by 5AM to fortify them on their journey. While the men filled up on fish cakes, beans, Potato Bargain and eggs, fish bones would be simmering on the wood stove; Emma would have chowder ready when they came in for lunch.

"I can see my Uncle George, 'Two Deer,' as clearly as if he were standing right here on the trail with us today. He always wore those khaki pants with lots of pockets. He'd go off into the thicket, stomping and beating the woods, barking like a dog. A group of eight or ten hunters would have gathered downwind along the trail and Uncle George would flush the deer in their direction."

Lost in memories of yesteryear, Earl continued walking in silence until he came to a clearing. The land fell away, forming a slight valley. Overhead trees formed a canopy as they reached out to others on the other side of the glen.

Stopping in his tracks, he asked, "What is this?" I shook my head.

"This is creation," Earl said, answering his own question. "It's all right here—Father Sky, Mother Earth, Brother Wind, wildlife, marine life. See how Yotannit (the Spirit of the Sun) greets us with light and warmth trickling through the branches. This is what it's all about. I don't need a building. When people say that trees don't talk, it means that they don't listen; they just don't hear. These trees tell me how many moccasins have passed by here. That rock guides me along the path; the moss growing on its north side tells me the directions. The wind calls me."

In the woods, along the winding path, I discovered a new perspective on hunting and was reminded of how Earl's people revere the Earth and its creatures. Never would they take more than they needed for sustenance. Never would they fail to give thanks for such gifts.

FRICASSEED RABBIT

1 rabbit
1 gallon salted water
4 tablespoons vinegar
1 cup flour
2 teaspoons salt
1 large onion, chopped
2 carrots, chopped
3 celery stalks, chopped
2 medium garlic buds, chopped
1 bay leaf
salt and pepper to taste

Sauce:
3 cups stock (use stock from
   stewing rabbit supplemented
   with prepared stock if necessary)
2 tablespoons butter or margarine
2 tablespoons flour
salt and pepper to taste

Soak the rabbit for at least 1 hour (preferably overnight) in the salted water with the vinegar. Drain and rinse thoroughly.

I prefer to fry the rabbit before fricasseeing. Browning the rabbit improves the flavor and appearance. Cut meat into serving size pieces and dust in a paper bag that contains a cup of flour and 2 teaspoons salt. Using a sauté pan, fry rabbit until brown on all sides.

Put browned rabbit in a pot, cover with water and add the onion, carrots, celery, garlic, bay leaf, salt and pepper.

Bring to a boil. Turn down to a simmer and cook, covered, for 1–1½ hours, or until tender. Remove the rabbit pieces. Save, strain and measure 3 cups of the stock.

Make a roux of butter or margarine and flour, cooking until the mixture resembles corn meal. Add 2 cups of stock, whipping and getting into the corners of the pan with a rubber spatula. Bring to a boil again and add more stock if consistency is too thick. Sauce should coat a spoon. Add salt and pepper to taste.

Return to pot containing rabbit pieces. Heat and serve.

Optional method for boneless fricassee

Remove meat from the bone, preserving large pieces wherever possible. Strain the stock and thicken. Put meat into stock. If stock is too thick, add some of the remaining stock.

Reheat and serve with rice or mashed potatoes, squash and cornbread.
Serves 4–5.

FRIED RABBIT

1 rabbit
1 large onion, chopped
2 carrots, chopped
3 celery stalks, chopped
1 bay leaf
2 medium garlic buds, chopped
salt and pepper to taste

Sauce:
4 tablespoons margarine
3 tablespoons flour
2–3 cups stock (use stock from
    stewing rabbit supplemented
    with prepared stock if necessary)

Place the rabbit in a large saucepan and cover with water. Add onion, carrots, celery, bay leaf, garlic, salt and pepper and bring to a simmer. Cook until tender, approximately 1–1½ hours. Remove rabbit from the pot and allow to cool.

Melt 4 tablespoons margarine in a pot. Add 3 tablespoons flour and start whipping over a medium heat. Add 2 cups of strained stock, continuing to whip to get the roux from the corners of the pan. Bring to a boil. Sauce should coat a spoon. If it's too thick, add a little more stock.

Cover the bottom of a large skillet with oil and place over a medium heat. Dust the rabbit by placing it in a paper bag with flour and a little salt. Fry the rabbit until done. Drain on paper towels. Serve with the sauce.

Serves 4–5.

RACCOON

1 raccoon	4 celery stalks
1 large onion, chopped	2 bay leaves
2 carrots, chopped	1 cup vinegar

Soak raccoon in cold, salted water overnight. Drain and rinse thoroughly.

Cut into serving size pieces and place in a 2-gallon pot. Cover with water and add the vegetables, bay leaves, and vinegar. Bring the water to a boil. Turn down to a simmer, cover and cook until tender, 1–1½ hours.

Preheat oven to 425°. Remove meat from stock. Arrange the pieces of meat on a wire rack in a roasting pan, and place the pan in the middle of the oven. Add enough stock to the pan to cover the bottom, but not enough to cover the rack (about two large ladles of stock). Bake for 45 minutes to one hour, turning the pieces at 10–15 minute intervals. "Coon" is done when it is crispy, has been turned and is browned on all sides. It can be eaten with or without sauce.

Serves 6.

Earl's granddaughters Equa Mills and Madas Pocknett in front of photos of ancestors.

The Ockrey Trading Post

Like the name of the town itself, all of our names came to be changed over the years. Ours somehow evolved from Ochree to Ockrey and eventually to Oakley. My great grandfather was George Ockrey. His son, Irving Oakley—"Mr. Irving" to the kids and "Quack" to the adults—was the original owner of the trading post. Grandmother Christine served the local community as the midwife and herbalist and was considered an official *saunks*, or woman chief. Her home in the center of town was open to everyone. It's been said that she had a "stingy table," meaning there was never enough room for everyone who came by. Christine and Irving were the parents of Ellsworth, "Drifting Goose," who became the Sachem and whose son later became the Supreme Sachem, or chief, and took the father's name, "Drifting Goose."

The Ockrey Trading Post, named after my great grandfather, was always the sentimental center of town. Townsfolk congregated inside or on the steps to socialize and swap stories. The store wasn't always open for business, but that didn't deter children coming to buy penny candy. They'd go up the path to my grandparents' house on the hill and holler, "Store!" Mr. Irving would come out in due time to serve the children, and he wasn't always thrilled about being interrupted. He'd come out when he was dog-gone good and ready, mumbling and cussing all the way down the hill to the store to wait on kids who'd probably be spending about a penny each.

Since many people had no well or pumps back then, they'd come to Ockrey to get water from the town pump and horse trough located just outside the store, which also had an apple orchard, a barn and a smokehouse out back. Hunters would come to the barn with their deer (out of sight of the game warden). There they skinned and gutted them then let them hang to age. The meat wasn't actually sold at the store, but instead divided up and shared throughout the small, rather clannish community, which numbered about 350 people during the '30s and '40s.

Cynthia "Tinny" Hammond was a robust woman and an excellent cook who rented the trading post from my mother after Grandpa passed on. She added a lunchroom called the Silver Moon with a soda fountain and a jukebox where we learned to dance. She loved having a place where kids could hang out. We only sat down in the wire-backed ice cream parlor chairs when we weren't dancing. Boy, I can still hear that old juke box playing my favorite song, Charlie Barnett's "Cherokee."

Years later, my brother Elwood came home from World War II and took over the store from my mother, working alongside his wife Josephine. He, my father and several other tradesmen expanded the upstairs and added dormers to make living space for himself, his wife and their three children.

Elwood was a most proficient hunter, bringing home rabbits, raccoons, partridge, quail, an occasional woodcock, duck or deer—maybe even a skunk. It wouldn't bother Elwood one bit to close the store and hang a "Gone Fishin'" or "Gone Huntin'" sign on the door. It wouldn't bother the townspeople either, for they know he is of the land and belongs to the land. Indians have always spoken of the land and all of creation with genuine courtesy and respect. We have no need or desire to control any part of the circle of creation. The land, and especially any place where we live or have lived, is one with our people and our ancestors.

The Ockrey Trading Post, 1937. Drawing by Shirley Peters.

DOMESTIC MEAT & POULTRY

GIFTS OF THE SACRED LAND

The first recipe in this section comes from my good friend, Adrian Yelle, former executive chef of the Popponesset Inn. He is a brother in spirit, my mentor and the epitome of gentility. In many ways, Adrian brings to mind my older brother who was killed in World War II. I think the resemblance has much to do with a special kinship Adrian and I developed.

I worked with Adrian at the Popponesset Inn in the late forties shortly after I was discharged from the service. As head chef at "Poppy," Adrian oversaw the entire operation. Back in the days when "royal treatment" was merely another ingredient in the dining experience, Adrian tended the gardens, arranged the flowers, and planned the menus around carefully selected produce, fish and meat. His legendary buffets featured innovative and attractive salads, pastas, fruit, seafood and meats flanked by his own creative floral adornments. The menu varied, but Adrian's attention to detail was evident in the turkeys and hams as well as in his special dishes. Hot buttered potato salad, Lobster Newburg and Chicken Tetrazzini appeared along with baked beans and my sister Delscena Hendricks' fabulous desserts.

Each day we'd check to see what we had on hand before deciding on a menu. Adrian was a genius at combining spices and seasonings and perfecting old favorites. Recipes were merely a basis for research; he could improve on anything. Each dish reflected his ingenuity and creativity.

I never see a buffet table without thinking of Adrian's, and they never compare favorably with his. In fact, many of the things I cook today remind me of Adrian. I'm grateful that I had the opportunity to work with such a fine gentleman, and I'll always value his expertise and advice.

Earl with Adrian Yelle.

BONELESS ROAST OF VEAL
with Watercress Stuffing & Champagne Sauce
(from Adrian Yelle, former chef, Popponesset Inn)

1 3-pound leg of veal, boned & tied
butter, enough to cover veal, softened
salt and pepper to taste
½ cup carrots, chopped
1 cup onions, chopped
1 cup celery, chopped
1 bay leaf
½ teaspoon thyme
2 cups chicken broth
split of champagne
cornstarch and flour, mixed, for
    thickening sauce

Stuffing:

4–5 cups dried Portuguese bread,
    cubed
2 cups chicken broth
½ cup onion, chopped
½ cup celery, chopped
½ teaspoon sage
¼ pound butter
Salt and pepper to taste
bunch of watercress, chopped
    coarsely, without stems

Preheat oven to 350°.

Coat veal generously with soft butter. Sprinkle with salt and pepper. Place on rack in roasting pan.

Combine carrots, onions, celery, bay leaf, thyme and 2 cups of chicken broth. Pour mixture over meat then roast for 30 minutes. Turn roast, reduce heat to 300°, and roast for another two hours, basting frequently. After first hour, baste with one split of champagne.

While roast is cooking, prepare the watercress stuffing. Mix Portuguese bread, broth, onion, celery, sage, butter and salt and pepper to taste in a small pan. Cook five minutes. Add the bunch of watercress. Toss with stuffing mixture. Place in small casserole and bake with roast for 30 minutes.

When roast is cooked, remove and strain the broth from pan. Thicken broth slightly with flour and cornstarch mixed. If necessary, add more chicken broth to sauce.

Serves 8.

POT ROAST

3–3 ½ pounds bottom round cut
   pot roast
oil
water to cover
1½ cups onions, chopped
1 cup celery pieces
4 buds garlic, smashed
2–3 bay leaves

Gravy:
2 cups stock
2 teaspoons salt (adjust to taste)
½ teaspoon pepper
2 teaspoons base or 2 bouillon
   cubes (adjust salt accordingly)

flavor additive (e.g., Gravy Master
   or Chef Bouquet)
2–3 tablespoons cornstarch* with
   enough water or stock to mix
   thoroughly
optional: ½ cup each carrots, celery,
   onions and green peas, several
   sliced white mushrooms
   *I prefer to use cornstarch rather than a
   roux in this clear sauce simply because it
   allows the grain of the meat to show
   through rather than masking the meat.*

Select a pot big enough to hold the meat. Brown pot roast on all sides, starting with the fat side down, in just enough oil to keep meat from sticking to the pan.

Add enough water to completely cover the roast. Add the onion, celery, garlic and bay leaves. Bring to a boil. Turn down to a simmer. Cover and let simmer for an even three hours. Add water as necessary to keep meat covered. Remove meat carefully to prevent roast from breaking apart.

To make the gravy, first strain the stock. Discard the vegetables. Bring stock to a simmer. Add salt and pepper to taste, base or bouillon and flavor additive. Add cornstarch mixture and blend thoroughly.

To carve the roast, if it is still hot, use a very sharp knife and slice across the grain of the meat. If the corner of the roast appears to shred or crumble, flip the roast over and slice in the same direction on the other side. Crumbled pieces can be used for hash.

For Optional Jardiniere Gravy
Julienne carrots and celery. Cube onions. Bring strained stock to a simmer then blanch vegetables in stock. Add salt and pepper to taste, base or bouillon and additive. Add cornstarch mixture and blend thoroughly. Add peas and sliced white mushrooms, if desired, before serving.

Serves 8.

NEW ENGLAND BOILED DINNER

3 pounds red or gray corned beef
  (I prefer gray)
2½ quarts water
6 bay leaves
6 to 8 medium potatoes, peeled, not
  cut
1 medium head of cabbage, cut into
  6–8 pieces

8 to 10 carrots, peeled and cut into
  chunks
salt and pepper to taste
3 to 4 tablespoons melted butter
bunch of parsley
optional: beets, turnips, onions

Cut the corned beef across the grain into 2 or 3 small sections. Place in a large pan and cover with 2½ quarts of water and the bay leaves. Cook until the fat is softened, about 2½ to 3 hours. Remove the meat to a platter with a slotted spatula, reserving the water. Remove some of the water to a smaller pan for the carrots.

Bring the original pan of cooking water to a boil and add the potatoes and a little salt, tasting the water for saltiness first as corned beef can be salty. After 7–8 minutes, add the cabbage to the same water and cook for an additional 10 minutes until the core of the cabbage is soft. Meanwhile, in a separate pan, cook the carrots for 10 to 12 minutes, using the water you reserved for that purpose. If using turnips and/or onions, cut into pieces the same size as the carrots and add to the pan with the carrots. Beets should be cooked separately.

Place some of the cabbage on a platter, then slice the meat and place over the cabbage. Surround with the potatoes, carrots and remaining cabbage, and turnips and onions, if using. Top potatoes with melted butter and parsley. Beets should be placed directly on the serving plate.

Serves 6–8.

— · — · — · — · — · — · — · — · — · — · —

If you want to make hash with leftover meat, such as pot roast, boil extra potatoes while you're doing the roast. Process the cooked meat and potatoes in a grinder if you have one. If not, chop them up and add a little salt and pepper and a dash of light cream or milk for moisture to help browning. Melt butter in a preheated black cast iron "spider" and add the hash. Shape the hash and shake the spider to allow the hash to brown nicely. Turn out onto a hot platter. This is another full meal. Some folks like a poached egg, sliced beets or stewed tomatoes with hash.

— · — · — · — · — · — · — · — · — · — · —

RED FLANNEL HASH

leftovers from a New England boiled   butter
   dinner (*See* previous page.)   horseradish
light cream

Slice the leftover meat and heat in the broth from the boiled dinner.

Meanwhile, mix the leftover vegetables—cabbage, beets, carrots, potatoes, etc.—and chop coarsely in a wooden bowl with a hand chopper. Season to taste and add a little light cream to moisten and help brown.

Melt butter in a preheated black cast iron 'spider' and add the vegetable mixture. Shape the hash and shake the spider to allow the hash to brown nicely. Turn out onto a hot platter. Serve the meat separately or added to the hash.

Garnish with horseradish. For a horseradish sauce, add horseradish to cream sauce, or add horseradish to equal parts of mayonnaise and mustard.

Serves 6.

MEAT LOAF

Everyone's meat loaf is different, very often a concoction that has evolved over the years. There are as many methods as there are cooks.

2 pounds hamburger
¼ cup onion, chopped
¼ cup celery, chopped
¼ cup green bell pepper, chopped
½ cup bread crumbs
2 tablespoons A-1 sauce
½ tablespoon garlic powder
   OR 3 large garlic buds, minced

1½ teaspoons salt
½ teaspoon black pepper
4 slices bread
½ cup broth, stock or water
optional: creole or other tomato-
   based sauce for topping

Preheat oven to 350°.

Place meat in a large bowl. Add onion, celery, green pepper, crumbs, A-1, garlic and salt and pepper. Mix thoroughly by hand. Place bread on top of the mixture and soak with the broth or water. Squeeze bread so that any excess liquid will be absorbed into the meat mixture then mix bread into mixture. Shape meat into a firm loaf in a medium-sized baking dish, or make two smaller loaves and freeze one (uncooked) for later use. Bake 40–45 minutes. If frozen, cook for one hour or defrost in refrigerator before baking.

If desired, add creole sauce or some other tomato-based sauce to the top of the meat loaf for the last 10–15 minutes of cooking.

Serves 8.

STEW

2 tablespoons olive oil
1½ cups onions, chopped
1 pound stew meat*, trimmed
3 cups carrots, julienned
1½ cups celery, cubed
4 medium potatoes, cut into
    chunks
6 cups water or stock
1 bay leaf
optional: parsnips (bite size), mush-
    rooms, peas, pea pods, and
    dumplings

*Some suggestions for making stews with various kinds of meat:
Chicken stew (Use thighs and legs.)
Ham stew (Use ham bone along with pieces of meat. Simmer meat on the bone with sautéed onions for 20 minutes before adding vegetables.)
Lamb stew (Use chunks of left-over lamb with bone and stock or gravy.)
Pot roast (Use stock or gravy with chunks of cooked meat.)
Venison (You may want to marinate venison before stewing. A simple marinade: ¹/₂ cup red wine, black pepper, 1 bay leaf

Using a pan large enough to hold all ingredients, sauté onions in 1 table-spoon olive oil until brown. Remove onions. Add the rest of the olive oil to the pan and brown the meat on all sides.

Return the onions to the pan. Add carrots, celery and potatoes. Cover with water or stock. Cover the pan and simmer gently for 20–25 min-utes, or until potatoes are tender. Dumplings made with either flour or corn meal go well with stew; add them with 15 minutes left. If using mushrooms, add with 10 minutes to cook. Add peas or pea pods with 5 minutes left.

Serves 6.

CATHOLIC STEW
(from Jim "Choctaw" Brown)

This recipe originally comes from a former nun. In a New Mexico diocese, the nuns would prepare this weekly for any guests who may visit. Guests might include other nuns, priests, visiting dignitaries or parishioners. Initially, the stew was comprised primarily of leftovers. Eventually, New Mexican palates dictated its evolution.

1 pound chuck hamburger	4 large garlic buds, smashed
1 28-ounce can stewed tomatoes	1 15-ounce can kidney beans
chicken base or bouillon to taste	½ teaspoon crushed red peppers
½ cup celery, chopped coarsely	½ teaspoon cayenne
1 medium onion, chopped coarsely	¼ teaspoon black pepper

In a large pan, simmer hamburger in a little water until the water is gone and hamburger is rendered. Don't brown the meat. Drain fat and liquid, if any.

Add tomatoes and let them start "liking" each other a little bit. Add chicken base or bouillon mixed with a little water.

Taste. Add coarsely chopped celery and onion and smashed garlic. Cover and simmer on low heat. Keep veggies al dente. Add beans and seasonings. Bring to a slow simmer until meat is cooked.

Serve with Jalapeño Pepper and Cheddar Cheese Corn Bread. (*See* recipe on page 134).

Serves 6–8.

CREAMED DRIED BEEF

This is NOT your average "S.O.S." that was so unpopular in the armed services. Today we use a very lean beef, cut wafer thin. You can buy this beef at food wholesalers.

½ pound dried chipped beef
2 tablespoons butter or margarine
1–2 teaspoons dry mustard

⅛ cup dry sherry
2–2½ cups unsalted cream sauce
  (use recipe on p. 26, omitting salt)

If the dried beef is salty, separate the pieces of meat and soak them in warm water for a couple of minutes to remove some of the salt. This won't be necessary if good beef is used.

Using a medium-sized pan, melt the butter, add the dried beef and sauté enough to coat the beef. Add the dry mustard and sherry and continue to sauté until the sherry comes to a simmer. Add unsalted cream sauce.

Serve over toast points with a grind of black pepper.

Serves 4.

GOULASH

2 pounds Spanish onions, finely
  chopped
⅓ cup butter
2 tablespoons paprika
1⅓ pounds stewing beef, cut into
  2-inch cubes
salt to taste

1 garlic clove, chopped
½ teaspoon caraway seeds
⅓ cup plus 2 tablespoons red wine
⅓ pound green peppers, sliced
1 medium tomato

Fry the onion to a golden brown in butter in a large pan. Add the paprika and mix well.

Add cubed meat and brown in butter. Flavor with salt, chopped garlic and caraway seeds. Add the red wine, cover and braise on medium heat. (Add a little water to keep meat covered, if necessary.)

Before the meat is fully done, add the peppers and tomato. Simmer until meat is tender, making sure that there is enough liquid to cover the meat.

Serves 6–8.

STAY-A-BED STEW

(from Lisa Crowden)

1 pound stew meat*
1 can tomato soup
1 large potato, sliced
1 large onion, chopped
1 cup fresh carrots, sliced
1 can green beans with liquid

1 whole bay leaf (remove before
  serving)
1 cup water
salt and pepper to taste
  Beef, venison or any wild game

If using oven, preheat to 250°.

Place all ingredients in a 4-quart stew pot with a tightly-fitting lid. The stew will cook down, so more water may be needed.

Place in oven for 4–6 hours; cook on top of the stove in a covered stew pot for 3–4 hours; or cook all day in a crock pot. If you wish to speed up the cooking in the crock pot, heat water and soup before placing in the crock pot.

Serves 4.

HOG'S HEAD CHEESE

This is actually more like a luncheon meat than cheese. My father liked making and eating it. His favorite sandwich was hog's head cheese with mustard and mayonnaise.

hog's head, cut in two pieces
1 large onion, stuck with 3–4 cloves
3 celery stalks, halved
1 carrot, halved
4 large garlic cloves, smashed
4 bay leaves
4 tablespoons white vinegar

3–4 quarts water (enough to cover)
1 tablespoon dry mustard
2½ tablespoons salt
½ tablespoon black pepper
1–2 teaspoons poultry seasoning
¼ teaspoon cayenne pepper

Clean head thoroughly and put everything except the last four ingredients into a large, heavy pot. Cover with water, bring to a boil, reduce heat, and simmer for 2½–3 hours until the meat falls off the bone and the liquid has been reduced enough to develop a rich, gelatinous broth.

Remove the head from the broth and allow to cool. Cut the meat into bite-sized pieces and return to the broth. Bring to a simmer. Season to taste with salt, pepper and poultry seasoning and continue cooking for another five minutes. Add cayenne pepper to taste. (Reheating serves to mix the natural gelatin from the head thoroughly through the mixture so that, when the head cheese is chilled, it will slice without crumbling.)

Remove the meat with a slotted spoon or flat strainer spatula and place in loaf pans. Press meat into the pans to about 1½ inches from the top and cover with the broth. Refrigerate until jellied (about 48 hours). When very cold, cut in slices ¼-inch thick and serve as an appetizer or on a sandwich.

Serve with horseradish sauce, mayonnaise, mustard, etc.

Serves 16.

MOCK HOG'S HEAD CHEESE
"Headless Cheese"

Use all the ingredients in the previous recipe, but substitute the following
for the hog's head:

3 pounds fresh pork picnic
  shoulder, bone-in, or similar cut
2 pig's feet, split
  OR pork bones

1 pork tongue, if available
  OR a small cut of pork with bone

Place the meat, onions, celery, carrots, garlic, bay leaves, vinegar and dry mustard in water and bring to a boil. Reduce heat and simmer for 1½–2 hours.

Remove the pork shoulder and the tongue or pork meat and continue
simmering the feet for 1 additional hour to develop a rich, gelatinous
broth. Then remove all skin, bones and gristle and cut the meat into ½- to
¾-inch pieces and set aside.

Strain the stock, saving any remaining pieces of meat to chop up.
Season stock with the last four ingredients from previous recipe to taste.
Mix all the meats together and add enough of the strained seasoned stock
to cover. Return the mixture to the heat and return to a simmer for 2–3
minutes.

Continue directions from previous recipe.

Serves 8.

A Thanksgiving Story

Painting by Dr. Walton C. Galinat.
See page 122 for full description.

In 1621, when the Plymouth colonists celebrated their first Thanksgiving in America, about 90 Wampanoag Indians attended, bringing their traditional foods. This first Thanksgiving would not have been possible without the Wampanoags, for the seeds brought over the Atlantic did not grow well in the New World, and the pilgrims were actually in danger of starvation.

Instead, the large outdoor tables were filled with turkey as well as venison, duck, goose, clams, eel and other fish, wild plums, leeks, watercress and corn bread. Three days of feasting and games followed.

In subsequent years, the colonists learned from the Indians how to hunt and cultivate in this strange, somewhat harsh, but beautiful new place. Each year the New England colonists set aside a day for feasting and giving thanks, in remembrance of that first celebration. The custom spread and, in 1863, President Abraham Lincoln proclaimed the last Thursday in November to officially be a day of Thanksgiving across the United States.

ROAST TURKEY

1 turkey complete with giblets
optional:
   stuffing (*See* recipe, next page)
   OR 1 medium onion, quartered
   2 cups celery ends

salt
1/8-pound margarine, melted
1 pint water

Preheat oven to 350°.

Remove neck, giblets, etc. from the bird and rinse them and the cavity with salt and cold water. Set the neck and giblets aside for making gravy.

Place turkey, back side down, on a wire rack in a roasting pan. For a stuffed bird, stuff with your favorite stuffing (or use recipe on next page), or put a quartered medium onion and two cups of celery "ends" in the neck and stomach cavities, to help keep the turkey moist, along with a little salt. Drip melted margarine over the breast and drumsticks.

Add about a pint of water to the roasting pan to catch the drippings and to keep the pan from drying out. Cover with aluminum foil until the last hour. After the first half hour, baste the turkey every 30 minutes with the pan drippings.

Roast a large unstuffed turkey (up to 12 pounds) for approximately 3 hours. If the turkey is stuffed, it will take considerably longer. The turkey is done when the legs move up and down easily

Remove the bird from the pan to a platter and let rest for half an hour before carving.

A 12-pound turkey serves 8–12 people.

TURKEY STOCK

turkey giblets, organ meats, and
   neck
1 cup celery ends

1 medium onion for each turkey part
2–3 quarts water, enough for
   desired quantity of stock

Bring the meat, celery, onion and water to a simmer until the neck meat is falling off the bone—about 1½ to 2 hours. Keep water at the same level by adding hot water to the pot.

Strain and reserve the giblets, organ meats and neck. Chop up and add to gravy as desired.

TURKEY GRAVY

turkey bits and pieces from pan
¼ pound margarine and/or turkey
    fat
½ cup flour

2 quarts turkey stock
salt and pepper
optional: Gravy Master or other
    type of coloring, chicken base

When the turkey is removed from the roasting pan, scrape the bottom of the pan to gather up the brown bits and pieces. Add some of the stock if necessary to remove all of the bits from the pan. Strain this into the turkey stock.

Make a roux with the margarine and/or turkey fat combined with the flour. Thicken two quarts of the stock so that it begins to coat a spoon.

Chop the giblets and some of the neck meat and add to the gravy. Add salt and pepper to taste. Gravy Master or some other type of coloring may be added if needed along with some chicken base. Salt should be adjusted if base is used.

TURKEY STUFFING

1 loaf bread, cubed and dried out
1 large onion, chopped
4–5 stalks of celery, peeled and
    chopped
½ pound margarine
2 teaspoons salt (less if base is used)
½ teaspoon pepper (less if base is used)

1–1½ tablespoons poultry season-
    ing or sage
1 to 2 tablespoons parsley, chopped
optional: pecans, oysters, chopped
    neck meat and/or giblets, turkey
    or chicken base and/or stock

Cube the bread ahead of time, preferably, the night before, to let it dry out a little. Coarse bread makes better stuffing than sliced white bread, but either may be used.

Sauté the onion and celery in margarine until soft. If you add base to the onion and celery, use salt and pepper sparingly. Pour celery/onion mixture over the bread and fold in, adding parsley and poultry seasoning or sage to taste. Add optional ingredients. Stock may be used if you prefer a more moist stuffing.

Either stuff the bird or heat the stuffing in loaf pans. Remember that everything in the stuffing has already been cooked (unless you add oysters). If using loaf pans, baste with a little stock and cover with foil.

GIBLET OR LIVER PÂTÉ

Like most kids, I hated liver, but I loved my mother's pâté. She always prepared it in her black spider before we sat down. It was part of our dinner—a special accompaniment like banana fritters with syrup. The pâté was served warm on dry toast points. There was no chance that it would ever last long enough to cool and find its way onto crackers as an appetizer.

giblets, neck meat, gizzard, heart,
   liver, cooked or left over from
   making stock (*See* page 61.)
½ medium onion, chopped
1 stalk of celery, chopped
2 tablespoons margarine

1 egg
¼ cup mayonnaise
1 teaspoon salt
¼ teaspoon pepper
6 slices of bread, toasted

Chop or grind the giblets, neck meat, gizzard, heart and liver or liver only if making Liver Pâté. Sauté celery and onions in a spider or sauté pan with margarine until soft. Add chopped or ground meat to cooked celery and onions. Stir thoroughly.

Make a hole in the center and scramble the egg thoroughly. Stir the egg in until thoroughly mixed. Add the mayonnaise to the pan, mixing thoroughly (the pan will still be warm). Salt and pepper to taste.

Toast several slices of your favorite bread. Cut the dry toast into points, corner to corner, and serve with the pâté.

Serves 6 as an appetizer.

CHICKEN À LA KING

1 chicken breast
1 medium green pepper, cubed
12–14 whole fresh white
  mushrooms
1 cup pimento, in chunks
¼ cup dry sherry

Cream Sauce:
3 cups milk
6 tablespoons margarine
6 tablespoons flour
1½ teaspoons chicken base
¾ teaspoon salt
¼ teaspoon white pepper

Simmer chicken for approximately 30 minutes, until tender. Remove from water with a slotted spoon. Cool and cut into bite-size chunks.

Add the cubed pepper and mushrooms to a little water and simmer for 2–3 minutes. Remove immediately to prevent further cooking and set aside. Meanwhile, scald the milk in a double boiler over high heat. Turn heat to medium high and keep milk warm.

In another pan, melt the margarine and add the flour, stirring continually until the consistency resembles corn meal. Add ¾ of the scalded milk and heat the mixture to bubbling, continually whipping. Add the rest of the milk. Continue to whip, keeping mixture smooth and thick until it comes to another boil. Remove from heat.

Add the salt and chicken base, using salt sparingly. Taste for flavor. Fold in the chicken, chopped pimentos, mushrooms and peppers (minus the liquid) with a rubber spatula. Add the sherry and white pepper. The sherry will help bring out the chicken flavor. Sherry may be added or subtracted to taste, or to thin the cream sauce if it seems too thick.

Serve over toast points and garnish with a pineapple slice.

Serves 6.

CHICKEN DIVAN

6 cups water or stock
2 chicken breasts, with skin on
½ cup onion, chopped
½ cup celery pieces
2 garlic buds, smashed
1 large bunch broccoli
8 tablespoons butter or margarine
½ cup flour
2 teaspoons salt*
½ teaspoon white pepper

¼ cup Parmesan cheese
¼ cup bread crumbs
optional: Light cream,** 15–20
    mushrooms, 2 teaspoons chicken
    base/bouillon
    *If using chicken base and/or bouillon
    cubes, reduce the salt.*
    **Add light cream for a richer sauce or
    to increase the amount of sauce.*

Preheat oven to 350º.

Bring water or stock to a boil. Add whole chicken breasts, onion, celery and garlic. Simmer until firm and tender (15–20 minutes). Remove pan from heat.

Trim broccoli; cut off florets, clean and peel the stem. Slice the stem in long pieces, rotating and cutting so that slices are on the diagonal and not symmetrical in size or shape (Chinese cut). The different shapes and sizes add to the esthetics and the texture of the dish. Blanch broccoli florets and pieces in boiling, salted water (3–5 minutes). Remove immediately. Cool if necessary to retard further cooking. If using mushrooms, cut them in half and plunge them into the same water to blanch.

Strain chicken stock into a pot and bring it to a simmer. Meanwhile, skin and bone the chicken, remove any fat and cut into cubes. Make a roux with the flour and butter or margarine. Add to simmering stock and whip until thickened. Add salt and pepper, as well as chicken base or bouillon and light cream, if using. Layer in a medium size baking dish— sauce, broccoli, mushrooms, chicken, sauce. Sprinkle Parmesan cheese and bread crumbs over sauce.

Bake for about 30 minutes until bubbly and brown.

Serves 8.

CHICKEN TETRAZZINI

2 chicken breasts, with skin on
6 cups water
½ onion, chopped
½ cup celery pieces
2 buds of garlic, smashed
½ pound spaghetti
4 teaspoons salt*
dash olive oil
12 medium white mushrooms,
    halved

1 stick, margarine (8 tablespoons)
½ cup flour (scant measure)
¼ cup Parmesan cheese
¼ cup bread crumbs
¼ teaspoon white pepper
optional: 1 tablespoon chicken base
    *You may want to use less salt when
    using chicken base.*

Preheat oven to 350°.

Place chicken breasts in a medium saucepan with water, onion, celery and garlic. Bring to a boil. Turn down to a simmer. Cook chicken until firm and tender, 15–20 minutes. Turn off heat and set pan aside.

Break spaghetti into four pieces. Undercook spaghetti in boiling water with 2 teaspoons salt and a dash of olive oil. Strain spaghetti and place in baking dish.

Add a little water or chicken stock to a saucepan and bring to a boil. Blanch the mushrooms for 15–20 seconds. Drain and add to spaghetti.

Remove chicken and strain liquid into a saucepan. Skin, bone, and dice chicken and place on top of the mushrooms.

Make a roux of the margarine and flour and cook until the texture resembles corn meal. Bring the reserved chicken stock to a boil. Add the white pepper, the additional 2 teaspoons of salt (or less salt if using chicken base) and the roux, continually whipping until the sauce begins to thicken. Pour the stock over the chicken, mushrooms and spaghetti using a rubber spatula to get the sauce out of the pan and down between the ingredients. Add Parmesan cheese and bread crumbs.

Bake for 25 to 30 minutes.

Serves 6.

CHICKEN WILLIAM

1 chicken breast, boned and
  skinned
1–2 tablespoons olive oil
1 tablespoon butter

6 medium mushrooms, sliced
¼ cup vermouth or dry sherry
optional: Pea pods, julienne carrots

Sauté chicken in oil. Cover and cook until almost done. Drain oil.

Add butter. Sauté chicken and mushrooms (and pea pods and carrots, if using) until chicken is coated in butter and has picked up some color. Add vermouth or sherry. Cover and simmer for another 2–3 minutes.

Place on plate and pour sauce and mushrooms over the chicken. If using pea pods or carrots, remove them with a serving spoon. Place the carrots on one side of the breast and the pea pods on the opposite side.

Serves 2.

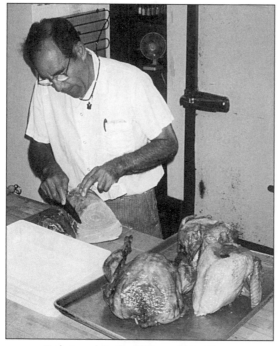

Earl at work in the kitchen of The Flume.

SEAFOOD

SPRING (Se-quan-an-kees-wush, When they set the corn)

Our constant challenge with nature and the outdoors is balanced in springtime by the miracle of new life. In the spring when the sun is a little warmer, the herring and white perch begin their long runs, and trees and shrubs begin to sprout. There is a general awakening everywhere.

When we were young, mayflowers were special to us because they signaled spring and because we made money selling them in front of our house. Being careful not to pull up the whole plant, we'd pick the best of the dainty flowers. Then we'd rush home and arrange them in bouquets that we'd place in a large vase of water. Cars would stop on their way through our little town and folks "from away" would pay 15 cents for the fragrant bouquets. We'd sell them all by noontime. I loved to present my mother with a bunch of lilies of the valley. My own favorite flower was the lady slipper, which we called "Squaw Moccasin."

Soon it would be May Day, a time for honoring the elders in the community with May baskets. Local merchants would save boxes for us kids, and we'd decorate them with crepe paper and ribbons held on with lots of glue made from flour and water. We'd fill the baskets with hard candy and home-baked goods. Even as kids, we all baked. It was great fun to knock on the doors of the elders' homes, leave the baskets and run away.

Spring was also time to fix the grape arbor, trim the fruit trees and plant the early vegetables like lettuce and peas. Peas would have to be ready for the Fourth of July for the traditional salmon and peas. Mr. George Avant would come by to till the garden with his horse and plow. It was a treat to watch the plow being pulled and the earth prepared after its long winter nap.

Poles as straight and thin as rods were set in the ground for the pole beans. My father was a stickler that this be done just right. He'd store the

Fishing boat docked at Olin Kelley's Waquoit Shellfish.

poles from year to year in the crotch of a tree or he'd cut new ones. I remember him sitting in the kitchen and cutting the eye from a potato to plant in the garden along with his beets, tomatoes, onions, carrots, squash and corn. The squash and corn would be tied to the beans to unite the Three Sisters.

Living off the land as we did required careful attention to the elements. We wouldn't eat game or waterfowl in the spring when the weather wasn't cold enough to keep them healthy. In spring the only fresh meat available to us was skunk, which also served another purpose. The oil of the skunk was rendered for chest colds and coughs and was also used as a skin lotion.

The herring run is a rite of spring. It's always a thrill to introduce people from away to this annual trek of the herring, as they make their way from the cold sea to spawn in area ponds. Their appearance on my own turf has been a constant welcome sight in my life for as long as I can remember.

Temporary homes would be set up along the rivers, bays and estuaries along the southwestern side of the Cape in Waquoit, Menauhant, West Falmouth and Popponessett. These were the places where we caught the herring and white perch as they returned to spawn in the ponds and lakes of their birth.

I was never more energized by the change in climate than in spring. This was also the time to select the sites for the hunting "blinds" that would be utilized in the late fall and early winter for duck and goose hunting.

Fishing was my all-time favorite pastime. As soon as the worms appeared, it was time to fish for trout in the Santuit and Mashpee Rivers. Trout fishing was exciting and fun because the trout is the smartest of fish. Hatched and born in the river, trout know the dark places to hide from fishermen. The chief of the trout was easily spooked, so we had to use our best techniques to match his wits.

Before sunrise, we'd put on those old hip boots, grab a fly rod, pick a long, tapered, floating line with a #6 eagle hook (talon) and tie a can of worms on each of our belts. "If you get there too late, the fish'll already have had their breakfast," was one of my father's favorite warnings. The water was cold as *Bejeesus,* but the experience was exhilarating—the sunrise, the sound of the water bubbling in the river and the challenge of the trout combined to start the day off early with a quickening heartbeat.

Back then we were aware of the purity of the water. Natives would set up temporary camps for fishing, but they wouldn't contaminate the water by living permanently on the shores. People from away recognized that the fish we caught were better because of the pristine water. Strangers would come by asking to buy our catch, pan-sized fish called "fingerlings." We considered the fish more important than money. The fish was for us. Just thinking about that trout on the way home would whet my appetite.

A wise man once said that if every boy could go fishing, there'd be no delinquency.

Beach at Cape Cod.

GIFTS OF THE SACRED WATERS

Native people have served as guides on hunting and fishing expeditions for many generations, and my family has carried on this tradition. My grandfather, my uncles, my father, my brothers and I led many trips into the Sacred Woodlands in search of game and to the Sacred Waters for fish.

When my father taught me how to use my hands and fingers with the rod and reel and to fly cast, his lessons repeated the very techniques my grandfather had taught him. He retold Grandpa's stories about important men who came to Mashpee back in the days of the old Hotel Attaquin.

As a preteen, I'd be up before dawn getting my father's boat ready, drying it out and preparing the supply of bait for the men who had hired me for the day. Providing night crawlers, worms or hellgrammite bugs and baiting the hooks for the fishermen were important parts of the job of an Indian guide. On occasion, I'd even grab some salt pork from the supply in our cellar for bait. Boy, the pickerel loved that.

By daybreak, when the boat was prepared, I'd go back to meet the fishing party. Off we'd go, rowing across Santuit Pond for smallmouth bass, yellow perch or pickerel. Maybe we'd go to Mashpee Lake or Flat Pond for white perch, or to Moody's Pond ice fishing for pickerel.

Once in a while we'd catch pickerel that would be stuffed for dinna' that night. We'd also bring home yellow perch, hornpout, sunfish (which we called "punkin' seeds") and, occasionally, a smallmouth bass. I remember my mother throwing a shoe in our direction for good luck when we were on our way out the door to the local trout streams and ponds. We'd holler back, "Get the 'taters ready!" We'd often have two or three different kinds of fish at one meal.

There were mishaps, of course. Sometimes, in our early morning haste, my brother Elwood and I would pedal our bikes across sand pits or rocky roads with fishing rods dangling across the handlebars. We were thrown from the bikes more often than we'd like to remember. When we were old enough to drive, we'd throw the boat on the back of my father's Model A pickup. There were times when we'd forget to anchor the boat and it would fall off the truck as we bounced over bumpy dirt roads. It's hard to remember a time when we weren't racing the clock.

Rocky shoreline.

Thanks to our Mother, the Earth,
Who sustains and nurtures us.
And to the family of Spirits
Who guide and oversee us
In our communication
With the Great Mystery.

FISH

SENATOR EDWARD M. KENNEDY'S
BAKED STRIPED BASS
with Tomatoes, Scallions & White Wine

1 striped bass fillet (about 7 pounds)   ¼ cup parsley, chopped fine
½ cup white wine   salt
1 bunch scallions, chopped   pepper
2 tomatoes, peeled, seeded and
   diced into ½-inch pieces

Preheat oven to 400°.

Cut fish fillet into equal portions. Place on a baking pan and season.

Drizzle wine over all. Sprinkle chopped scallions and tomatoes over fish. Bake until fork tender, about 10–15 minutes.

Garnish with chopped parsley.

Serves 6.

Fluke and filleted bluefish.

FINNAN HADDIE
(Smoked Cod or Haddock)

6 pieces of finnan haddie (smoked   3 tablespoons butter
cod or haddock, 6–8 ounces each)   2 tablespoons flour
1 small onion, thinly sliced   pinch of salt for each serving
3 cups light cream

Preheat oven to 450°.

Poach finnan haddie in enough water to cover and soften the fish. Drain and remove any bones. Place in buttered casserole or pan large enough to hold fish in single layer. Lay onion slices on top.

Heat cream. Make a roux with butter and flour and add to cream. Let thicken and pour over fish.

Place under broiler for about thirty seconds, just long enough to blanch the onions. Bake just until cream starts to bubble, onions are browned and roux is cooked, about 10–12 minutes.

Serves 6.

Bounty from the sea.

BROILED SALMON

6 8-ounce salmon fillets with skin
   removed
¼ cup oil or melted butter (or a
   mixture of the two)

salt
¼ cup water
juice of ½ lemon (more if desired)
seasoned bread crumbs

Preheat oven to 425°.

Melt the butter or oil, or a combination, in a shallow baking pan large enough to hold 6 fillets.

Coat the top of the fillets with melted butter and place buttered side down in seasoned bread crumbs to coat. Place the fillets in the pan with crumb side up. Coat the bottom of the pan with water. Do not wet the crumbs. Salt the fillets to taste.

Place the pan in a preheated oven for 5–6 minutes. Baste with lemon juice and place under the broiler to brown and crust for 3–4 minutes longer. Fish should flake when done.

Serves 6.

Salmon fillet.

POACHED ATLANTIC SALMON

This is a New England favorite—especially around the Fourth of July—and is often served with the first fresh garden peas and butternut squash.

4–5 cups water
2 or 3 bay leaves
1 tablespoon vinegar
2 teaspoons salt
½ cup dry white wine
6 8-ounce salmon fillets

Egg sauce
3 tablespoons margarine
2 tablespoons flour
1 cup warm milk
salt and pepper to taste
2 eggs, hard boiled and coarsely cut
1 tablespoon chopped parsley
lemon wedges

Make sauce first. Melt margarine over low heat. Add flour and blend. Cook until mixture begins to look like corn meal, then add milk, stirring all the while. Cook and stir with a wire whisk until sauce is thick and smooth. Add salt, pepper and eggs. Set aside in top of double boiler to keep warm.

Simmer water, bay leaves, vinegar and salt in a large skillet. Add the wine and fillets and continue simmering until fish is firm to the touch. Do not overcook. Remove fillets, let drain and place on heated plates, serving sauce on the outer third of the fish. Garnish with parsley and lemon wedges.

Serves 6.

SALMON & PEAS

2 15-ounce cans salmon, in water
  (fish stock)
4 cups milk
6 tablespoons margarine
5 tablespoons flour
2 teaspoons salt
½ teaspoon pepper

1 cup water
2 cups frozen peas
½ teaspoon sugar
optional: Fresh salmon and peas
  may be used, but this requires
  more work, time and expense for
  this simple and delicious dish.

Remove the skin and bones from the salmon, keeping the fish in large pieces. Reserve the liquid (fish stock). Bring the milk to a simmer.

Make a roux of the margarine and flour, cooking until it reaches the consistency of cornmeal. Add the heated milk to the roux, stirring with a wire whisk and using a rubber spatula to get the roux from the bottom and sides of the pan. Remove from the heat. Add 1½ teaspoons salt and the pepper, the reserved fish stock and large pieces of fish. Fold in the rest of the fish.

Place one cup of water, the remaining ½ teaspoon of salt and ½ teaspoon of sugar to a saucepan and bring to a simmer. Add peas. Simmer for two minutes. Reserve the water and add the peas to the fish mixture. Use water to thin the salmon/peas mixture if necessary.

Serve over toast points with baked potatoes.

Serves 6.

BAKED SCROD

6 tablespoons butter or oil
1 cup cracker or bread crumbs
6 6–8-ounce scrod (cod) fillets
salt

½ cup water
lemon juice
1 recipe Newburg Sauce (*See* recipe on page 29.)

Preheat oven to 450°.

Melt butter in a baking pan. Place crumbs on waxed paper. Coat each piece of fish on the top side with melted butter or oil. Then dredge in crumbs, adding a couple of shakes of salt over each fillet.

Put a small amount of water in the baking pan—about ½ cup, just enough to slightly film the bottom of the pan—to keep the fish moist and prevent it from sticking to the pan. Gently place the fish in the pan, separating the pieces so that they don't touch. Don't get water on the crumbs.

Bake for about 7–8 minutes. As soon as the crumbs begin to brown, squeeze a little lemon juice on each piece. Fish should be flaky and firm. Gently lift the edge of the fish with a wide spatula to test doneness. If the fish is sticking to the dish, add a little bit of water to the dish, not to the fish. Scrod may be placed under the broiler if it's not brown enough. Do not turn the fish!

Serve with Newburg Sauce. (*See* recipe on page 29.)

Serves 6.

— · — · — · — · — · — · — · — · — · — · — · —

Every Sunday morning my father would make his idea of a good, substantial breakfast—fish cakes and beans. He'd use a serving spoon and a fork to shape the fish cakes, always repeating the important information that you shouldn't use your hands to shape the cakes. He'd dip the spoon into the fish cakes to fill it up, smooth it over with the fork, even the mixture all around then push it into the pan and flatten it with the fork. "Just add oil as needed," he'd say, "you're not deep frying 'em." My mother always said that Ferdinand's fish cakes were so light they'd just fly right out of the pan.

There'd be no tasting those fish cakes 'fore they were ready. Emma would be sitting with her hands around a cup of coffee and getting tired of waiting; having the luxury to sit and be waited on was a rare occasion and she'd be getting hungry. "Well, Ferdinand," she'd say, "are those fish cakes ready yet? I've been waiting a long time."

He'd just move the pan, his entire being focused on the hot spot on the stove as if he had a fishing rod in his hand chummin' for that "Chief of the Trouts" that eluded him last time at Quashnet River, but there'd be no answer. He'd just keep moving the pan, shaking and rotating those fish cakes. We'd hear them getting crunchy and be pretty sure they were ready, but he'd take his time making sure that the edges were getting brown but never pressing them down.

And, when they were finally ready, they were always perfect. Worth the wait!

— · — · — · — · — · — · — · — · — · — · — · —

SALT CODFISH CAKES

½ pound salt cod
2 quarts water
½ cup onions, chopped coarsely
3 medium potatoes, cut in quarters
1–2 egg yolks
    OR one whole egg

¼–½ teaspoon black pepper
vegetable oil
Important: **Don't wash salt off codfish.**

Cut the codfish across the grain into small pieces. Boil in 2 quarts water until tender.

Add onions and potatoes to codfish and cook until potatoes are done, keeping level of water constant. Strain potato/codfish mixture completely. Return to pot. Mash thoroughly, adding egg yolk(s) or whole egg and pepper. Egg yolks make the fish cakes lighter.

Shape fish cakes and sauté in hot skillet with vegetable oil. Lower heat when nicely browned and continue to cook, turning often to ensure a thick brown crust.

Serves 4.

— · — · — · — · — · — · — · — · — · —

I remember my dad bringing home a washtub full of squirming eels and placing it in the kitchen. The eels were very slippery from all of their slime. My father would say, "Okay, boy, go get some newspaper."

He'd put on his leather apron in preparation for the skinning. Then he'd take out his whetstone, get the jackknife razor sharp and gut each eel. He'd take his thumb, run it down the backbone and remove the blood line under the filament of the belly. Then, holding the eel by its head, he'd cut pretty much through the backbone and then start to separate the head and skin from the back flesh of the eel.

He'd take that jackknife to the back of the head and get the skin started. Then, with a piece of the newspaper protecting each hand, he'd grab that little piece of the backbone with one hand and the skin with the other hand, pulling in opposite directions until the flesh came right out like a snake shedding its own skin. As he pulled it out, the eel would still be squirming. It wouldn't be alive, of course, but it would still squirm right around his arm.

— · — · — · — · — · — · — · — · — · —

EELS

4 eels   1 teaspoon salt for coating eels
¼ cup corn meal for coating eels   bacon fat (enough to sauté)
¼ cup flour for coating eels

Make a gash with a sharp knife across the length of the eel every inch or so. After three gashes, cut the eel all the way through to create a serving piece, then gash the other side. Gashing allows the eels to heat through and become crisp.

Make a mixture of corn meal, flour and salt and roll the pieces in the mixture to coat. Using the black spider frying pad, add a little bacon fat—not too much because the eels are oily—and let the black spider do its work.

Turn often and continue to cook until the eels are well browned.

Earl inside a dining room of The Flume.

Betty Reflects on the Annual Herring Run

The first time I saw a herring swim upstream, hesitate at the bottom and finally flip over the arduous crest and into the mill pond, I was reminded of the winner crossing the finish line of the Boston Marathon. The marathon was a rite of spring for me from the early 1950s, when I handed out oranges to the runners and waited until dusk for the last of the stragglers to pass by, to 1993 when I covered the race for a local newspaper.

On the other side of the Cape Cod Canal, the herring run heralds spring. While the runners are pooling on the common in Hopkinton, the strongest fish are hovering along the shores of Cape Cod awaiting their personal starting gun. What stimulus evokes the drive to return to the waters where were spawned three years earlier is their secret. Both runs involve a Herculean effort.

Veterans of this annual herring trek say that, in a good year, the river will turn black with fish and you can almost walk across the river on their backs. To those of us who wait out the New England winter, the swimmers and the racers are as welcome as the simultaneous arrival of pussy willows and the shad bush.

MARINATED HERRING

This marinade can also be used for eggs, pigs feet, mackerel or salmon.

12–24 herring
1 quart white vinegar
1½ cups (plus or minus) sugar
1½ cups water
1 tablespoon mustard seed
1 tablespoon peppercorns

1 tablespoon allspice
4–5 bay leaves
1½ medium onions, thinly sliced
2 lemons, thinly sliced
salt
optional: ½ teaspoon cloves

To make the marinade, combine all ingredients except the herring, onions and lemons in a medium saucepan. Bring to a boil and allow to cool. Taste for tartness.

Scale herring with a sharp paring knife. Then, with backbone toward you, cut out the fillet from head to tail. Turn over and cut from tail to head. Remove any roe from the fish and save for later use. Remove any large bones; smaller bones will be softened in the marinade.

Salt the bottom of a glass or crockery baking dish. Layer herring fillets, salting each layer, skin side down. Keep cool in cellar or refrigerate. Remove after 24 hours, brush with your hand to remove excess salt and place in glass, plastic or crockery. Cover with marinade. Add thin slices of lemon and onion. Keep cool in cellar or refrigerator. It will be ready to be served after 2 weeks.

Place a couple of herring on a bed of chopped lettuce and serve with a thin slice of red onion and sour cream, or serve as an appetizer on crackers or toast.

Serves 12–24 as appetizers.

HERRING ROE

36 pair herring roe*—good edible herring roe will be a yellow or orange color.
½ cup flour for coating roe
½ cup corn meal for coating roe
1½ teaspoons salt

¼ cup bacon fat or oil
Note: Shad roe, which has the same season, can be cooked in the same manner. Shad roe are larger; ½ pair is enough for each serving.

Mix equal parts of flour and corn meal—enough to coat the roe. Add a little salt.

Dredge the herring roe in flour and sauté in bacon fat (or your favorite oil) until coating browns. Turn and finish. Roe are delicate and cook quickly. Use oil sparingly.

Roe is typically served with a slice of bacon accompanied by a parslied potato and cream-style corn.

Serves 6.

Earl talking to young students at the herring run.

CORNED HERRING

Use a crock, plastic bucket or wooden barrel big enough to hold the herring. Cover the bottom of the container with salt. Rock salt is best, but regular salt or kosher salt will do. Place the herring tail to head and head to tail and belly to back and back to belly, covering each layer with salt. Store in a cool place (cellar, smoke house, refrigerator etc.), covered or uncovered for three days to "corn."

Next, pour cold, clear water over them and "slime" them in preparation for hanging them on the herring stick for storage and for eventual smoking. "Sliming" means pulling the herring through your hands to remove the excess salt, brine and albumin.

Corned herring can be baked or hung to dry on herring sticks for the eventual smoking process. Herring that will be baked should be refrigerated or frozen.

To bake the herring, preheat oven to 375°–400°. Line a baking sheet with a section of newspaper folded in several layers. Place herring on top of the newspaper, making sure that newspaper is covered by fish. Bake for about 20 minutes, until the tails break away.

Line a dinner plate with clean newspaper. Place cooked herring on the newspaper. Cut the head off. With a sharp paring knife, slit down the backbone under the skin and scales. Fold the flap back towards the belly, scraping the milt in with rest of the edible fish.

Pull the fish off in the direction of the bone to avoid getting small bones into the fish. Remove the backbone and eat the other half of the fish. If the herring has a good roe, eating the roe will be a bonus. It's delicious!

—▪—▪—▪—▪—▪—▪—▪—▪—▪—

My father was as much a part of the landscape as the seasons. Whether he was corning the herring, feeding the pigs or stringing the pole beans, he was "in the moment," as we say today. Whatever element he was in was where he was the happiest, where he was at his best. Attuned to the cyclical elements of life, he was deliberate in all of his actions; he was never rushed. Even if he were here with us today, he wouldn't look outside his own environment for entertainment, work, friends or sustenance.

—▪—▪—▪—▪—▪—▪—▪—▪—▪—

Ferdinand Mills and Charles Ayling getting ready to go fishing.

Smoking Herring

Let the salted herring (*see* recipe for Corned Herring, page 87) hang in the smoking area (house, old refrigerator, large bucket, etc.) for several weeks, until the surface of the herring begins to turn white from the salt. At about this time, the sweet fern will again appear in the woods after the long winter. These two signs will indicate that the herring are close to "gettin' the smoke."

Gather local wood. On Cape Cod we use sweet fern, apple, hickory, black alder and a little pine. Build a fire with some of the dry pieces of the branches and then smother it with the green pieces of fern, apple, hickory, alder and a branch or two of pine for color; maple can be used to get the fire going.

Don't allow the fire to become a blaze, because the fish will then be cooked and very susceptible to spoilage. Continue smoking for an hour or so, or until smoke dissipates. The smoking area can be aired out to let any heat out and to keep fish from cooking. Fish can be smoked at least once more or whenever wet or damp weather indicates mildew may be present. Damp, humid days are best for smoking because the smoke will tend to stay low and not dissipate.

A few days after the second smoking, pull off one of the herring, pick a cucumber from your garden and get the beer that is chilling in the refrigerator for this festive occasion and, as my father Ferdinand would say, "roll it inta' yuh."

SHELLFISH

CLAM CAKES

1½ cups flour
2 teaspoons baking powder
2 eggs
¼ cup milk
1 tablespoon lemon juice
2 cups clams (fresh or canned)

¼ cup clam broth (fresh or canned)
bacon fat or vegetable oil
optional: ½ teaspoon saffron, ½ cup
   minced onion, ½ cup broth and
   no milk

Sift dry ingredients together. Beat eggs in milk with lemon juice. Add clams, saving the broth. Add flour mixture and fold into beaten eggs and clams, adding broth. Make sure that the mixture isn't too wet.

Fry like pancakes in bacon fat. Clam cakes can be served with parslied potatoes, cream-style corn and rendered pork scraps and garnished with cucumber pickles.

Serves 6.

Clams and clam baskets.

WHITE CLAM SAUCE FOR PASTA

4 tablespoons cornstarch*
2 tablespoons water or quahog
  (hard-shell clam) juice (extracted
  in cooking process)
4–6 medium garlic buds, minced
1 tablespoon olive oil

12 quahogs (1½ cups)
juice of 12 quahogs (1½ cups)
1 cup parsley, chopped coarsely
ground pepper
  *optional: 2–3 tablespoons Parmesan
  cheese instead of the cornstarch and juice.*

Combine the cornstarch and water or juice. Soften the garlic in olive oil.
   Coarsely chop or grind the quahogs. Add them to the garlic and cook
until they are pale in color and the juice is extracted. Bring to a gentle
simmer (do not boil). Add parsley and simmer again. Add the juice and
bring to a slow simmer. Add the cornstarch mixture.
   Let thicken and pour over drained pasta. Add ground pepper to taste at
the table.

Serves 4.

RED CLAM SAUCE

Add your favorite red sauce (to taste) to the above recipe.

Serves 4.

WASHBOILER CLAMBAKE

This clambake is prepared on the top of the stove or on an outdoor grill. A washboiler is a large covered oval washtub. For a traditional campfire clambake (on the beach), see the details that follow this recipe.

2 dozen quahogs (hard-shell clams)
2 small chicken broilers, quartered
8 medium sweet potatoes, skin on, scrubbed
8 ears of corn, silk removed—husk left to cover corn
4 1½-pound lobsters
 OR 4 pounds of fish (sea bass, sea trout or white perch) with bone in, seasoned in cavity with salt and pepper.
8 small white potatoes, skin on, scrubbed
8 hot dogs

8 pieces of linguica (a Portuguese sausage),
 OR any local sausage
4 pounds soft-shell steamer clams
½ pound melted butter
2 quarts clam broth (extracted while cooking, supplement with canned if necessary)
1 medium watermelon, chilled
Salt and pepper
½ bag (bushel) rockweed,* kept wet
 *(If rockweed is not available, use wet lettuce that has been salted very liberally.)

Use 15 of the quahogs to make clam broth and the other 9 to line the bottom of the boiler or pot to create steam for the clambake. (These are not eaten as part of the meal; they are used here for their juice only, as the cooking tends to make them a little tough. The cook may snack on them or they may be saved to mince up for clam chowder.)

Make the clam broth first. Steam 15 quahogs with 4 cups of water in a pot with a cover, until quahogs open their shells and release all of their liquid. This should produce almost 2 quarts of clam broth. (Canned broth can be used.)

Season the quartered broilers with salt and pepper. Trim the corn by pulling back the husk, removing the silky threads and replacing the husk around the ears. Place all ingredients, except lobsters, in cheesecloth bags and tie loosely.

In the bottom of a washboiler or 8–10 gallon pot, place a thick layer of wet rockweed with half of the broth and add a pint of water. Layer the remaining quahogs on top of the wet rockweed and add another layer of wet rockweed.

Next, wrap the chicken in separate pieces of cheesecloth and tie loosely. Put them on the rockweed. Place eight medium sweet potatoes, with skin on, around the side of the chicken. Add the 8 ears of corn that have been trimmed for cooking. Add another layer of wet rockweed.

Place your choice of lobster or fish on top of the rockweed. I use a small sea bass, sea trout or white perch, cleaned with the bone in. Add among them 8 white potatoes, scrubbed with skin on. Add another layer of wet rockweed and pack the top of the boiler or pot with steamer clams, hot dogs and linguica. Add one or more layers of wet rockweed and the "bake" is complete except for the eating.

If the clambake is served in or near your home then, of course, the steaming can be done in your own kitchen. If you want a legitimate clambake with the "whole works" right down to the beach, cook the clambake out in the open on a grill.

Clambake is ready after 1½–2 hours of slow, steady cooking. When it is ready to be served, remove the cover from the boiler. Have a table ready from which to serve along with a cutting board and a sharp knife. Serve in the following order:

First course: Heat the clam broth and melt the butter. Discard the top layer of rockweed and serve each guest a portion of the soft-shell steamer clams. Serve a small cup of the piping hot clam broth for "washing" and melted butter for dipping. Be sure to save some of the butter and broth for the second and third courses. The clam is a finger food. Remove the clam from the shell and, at the same time, remove the loose black skin. Dip in the broth and butter.

Second course: On each plate serve a piece of the fish or half a lobster, a white potato, hot dog and linguica. Serve with some more of the butter.

Third course: Place a quarter broiler on each plate, along with an ear of corn and a sweet potato. Some of the melted butter and broth reserved from the earlier course will enhance the corn and sweet potato.

Fourth course: A slice of well-chilled watermelon is all you'll need to cap off the scrumptious clambake.

Serves 8.

Bakemaster Peter Hendricks, Earl's nephew, building the clambake by piling the food on in layers.

TRADITIONAL CLAMBAKE (APPANAUG)

Clambakes pre-date my earliest memories. Some of the people in my family who presided over clambakes as *bakemasters* were my father, my Uncle George Oakley and my brother-in-law, Milteer Hendricks. Remnants of old clambakes and stories of such festive occasions abound in Mashpee. Clambakes continue to mark special occasions, including the annual Mashpee Pow Wow.

On the day of a clambake, rockweed is collected. My family prefers to collect this greenish brown seaweed from the Cape Cod Canal at medium tide, because the swift current keeps the rockweed clean and free of algae. Rockweed grows in the crevices of rocks; its pockets hold saltwater.

Rocks are chosen for uniformity of size and shape. New rocks are required for each clambake since they lose *temper*, or their ability to hold heat, once they've been heated. The rocks are placed on the ground at the site chosen for the clambake.

One serving portion!

Traditionally, rocks were arranged in a circle, but in modern times the shape of the mound accommodates the shape of the firewood that is collected. Circles have special significance to my people, and it's easier to work with a circle since the food can be reached from every edge of the mound. However, in the photos in this book you'll see that the lengths of wood have determined the size and shape of the fire. The bakemaster determines when the rocks are ready and how long the fire will burn.

On the day of the bake, dry wood is piled on top of the rocks. A hose is always kept nearby to control the fire and keep the rockweed wet. Meanwhile, the food is prepared.

Clambake ingredients are wrapped in cheesecloth bags.

Bakemaster Peter Hendricks tending to the clambake.

Any unburned or partially burned wood is removed. Packets of foods are wrapped in cheesecloth and spread out over the rockweed and heated rocks as soon as the bakemaster announces that it's time. Follow the order of layers given below and the process outlined in the Washboiler Clambake recipe on pages 92 and 93. The chicken needs to be kept separate from the other foods and the fish wrapped in foil. You can use both fish and lobster.

Lobster is added later on top of a layer of rockweed that has been placed over the cheesecloth bags. It's very important to add a layer of wet rockweed between each layer of food. Steamers are added last over a thin layer of rockweed.

Rockweed covers everything. Today the entire mound is covered with polyurethane, and the people gathered around can see the food cooking and the lobsters changing from a cool blue to a deep warm red/orange. In the old days, a canvas was put over the mound.

The steamers break open and their juice, along with the moisture of the rockweed, is what steams the food. The food will take about an hour to cook. The bakemaster determines the proper cooking time.

Meantime, a table has been set up with the necessary serving utensils. The Quahog Chowder (*see* recipe on page 5.), broth and drawn butter are ready. When everything is in readiness, all the people gather in a circle of thanksgiving and the courses begin in the same order as we've listed in the Washboiler Clambake with just the addition of Quahog Chowder.

Bakemaster Peter Hendricks covering the clambake with rockweed.

LOBSTER NEWBURG

1 pound lobster	½ cup dry sherry
2 tablespoons butter	3 cups cream sauce (*see* recipe on
1 teaspoon paprika	page 26)

In a large saucepan, sauté lobster meat in the butter until the color begins to come off and meat is coated. Add paprika for color if needed.

Add half the dry sherry and simmer for 10–15 seconds, coating meat with the sherry. Add the necessary cream sauce to compliment the lobster meat. Bring to a simmer for 30 seconds. Add the remainder of the sherry to thin the sauce or add flavor if desired.

Serve with toast points and a garnish of fresh pineapple.

Serves 4 as an entree or 6 as a sauce.

MUSSELS

3 tablespoons olive oil (or mixture	5 pounds mussels
of olive oil and butter)	1½ cups white wine
6 small buds garlic, smashed	⅛ cup chopped parsley
¾ cup thinly sliced onions	buttered or Parmesan bread
¾ cup thinly sliced celery	

In a large saucepan, sauté garlic, onion and celery in olive oil. Lay mussels on top. Pour wine over mussels and cover tightly. Steam until shells open. Sprinkle chopped parsley over mussels.

Remove mussels from pan and place on serving dishes. Pour liquor from pan over mussels. Serve with crusty buttered or Parmesan bread.

Serves 6.

MUSSELS MARINIÈRE

4 tablespoons butter
4 tablespoons flour
1 teaspoon salt
¼ teaspoon pepper
¾ cup onion, chopped
6 small buds garlic, crushed
¾ cup celery, chopped fine

6 tablespoons butter
5 pounds mussels
1 cup white wine
4 tablespoons chopped parsley
1 teaspoon lemon juice
French bread

In a large saucepan, make a roux with the flour and butter. Season with salt and pepper. Set aside. Sauté onion, garlic and celery in butter. Lay mussels on top. Pour white wine over the mussels. Steam until shells open.

Strain liquid into the pot with the roux. Add parsley and lemon juice. Cook a minute or so. Pour over the mussels.

Serve with French bread.

Serves 6.

ESCALLOPED OYSTERS

1½ cups (25–30) oysters with their
    liquid
½ cup coarse cracker crumbs
    (saltines preferred)
½ cup melted butter

Pinch of salt
optional: dash of Tabasco, 1 table-
    spoon light cream, additional
    butter.

Preheat oven to 400°.

Stir cracker crumbs in butter to coat. Spread a thin layer in the bottom of a shallow baking dish.

Sprinkle oysters with a pinch of salt. Add oysters and some of the oyster liquid to the baking dish.

If light cream and Tabasco are used, mix them together and then drizzle over the oysters. Cover with remaining bread crumbs and bake for 20 minutes or until edges are bubbling and crumbs are nicely browned.

Garnish with parsley and lemon wedges.

Serves 6 as an appetizer or 2 as a main course.

OYSTER STEW

10–12 oysters, with liquid ½ teaspoon salt
1 tablespoon butter ½ teaspoon Worcestershire sauce
1½ cups milk or a combination of
   milk and cream

Sauté the oysters in the butter until the oysters curl at the edges. Add the milk. Bring to a simmer. Do not boil.

Add salt to taste and Worcestershire sauce. Serve in heated bowls with a grind of black pepper.

Serves 2.

SCALLOPS

This bivalve conjures up another time—a festive combination of camaraderie, competition, salesmanship and family meals. Scalloping is a way of life involving harvesting, shucking, selling the "catch" and, of course, eating. It's hard work and yet fun—one of many ways we celebrated community.

I was an adult before I ever saw sea scallops, which is what most people today refer to when they think of scallops. I prefer Cape scallops whenever they're available. They're more tender, more delicate and more flavorful than sea scallops. Long Island scallops are also good.

Sea scallops are larger than Cape scallops. You may want to cut them before cooking.

All scallops should be rinsed in cold salted water to remove sand and grit.

SCALLOPS IN THE RAW

The best way to eat scallops is as you are shuckin' them. Pull away the gut and eat 'em raw right off the knife.

SAUTÉED SCALLOPS

This is the second best way to eat scallops—almost as natural as eating them in the raw.

2½ pounds scallops (14–16 scallops per serving)
3 tablespoons flour
2 teaspoons salt
6 tablespoons butter
3 tablespoons oil

Shake flour and salt in a paper bag. Add scallops and shake the bag to coat and separate the scallops thoroughly. Rip open the bag and shake off any excess flour with your hands.

Preheat a large sauté pan, a black spider pan or a Teflon pan. A hot pan is required for fast cooking. Melt butter with oil added to keep the butter from burning at a high temperature.

When the oil spreads around the bottom of the pan, add the scallops. Shake the pan to cause the scallops to roll or roll them over individually with a fork. All sides don't need to be browned.

"Spoon" them onto heated plates when they're heated through.

Serves 6.

BREADED SCALLOPS

This is the third best way to prepare scallops.

2½ pounds scallops
4 tablespoons flour
2 teaspoons salt

1 cup milk
2 cups bread and/or cracker crumbs
1–2 cups vegetable oil

Dust scallops in flour/salt mixture, shaking to remove excess flour.

Place dusted scallops in milk to coat. Don't swish them around; this will remove the flour mixture. Remove the scallops carefully and let them drain well.

Place the scallops in the crumbs. Dry your hands and "bread" the scallops thoroughly, tossing them in the crumbs with your hands.

Heat the oil in a pan or deep fryer to 360°. Carefully add breaded scallops to the pan or to the deep fryer basket.

Fry until lightly browned. Drain on wet paper towels or paper bags. Serve immediately!

Serves 6.

Shellfish and boat at Olin Kelley's Waquoit Shellfish.

STUFFED SHRIMP

½ medium onion
2 stalks celery
19 large shrimp (U-10 or U-12 are
   good sizes)
10 tablespoons butter

1 cup crumbs
2 tablespoons sherry (plus more for
   "spraying")
optional: 2 medium sea scallops

Preheat oven to 450°.

Mince celery and onion. Add 4 tablespoons of the butter to a sauté pan and cook the onion and celery slowly to soften. Peel shrimp, leaving tail and first section intact. Split shrimp from second joint of the tail down the belly just to open and butterfly. Cut off all the little pieces of the end to keep the shrimp uniform in size. Set aside for use in the stuffing. If using scallops, chop them and one shrimp. Add, with any shrimp pieces, to the celery and onion mixture and continue to sauté for 2–3 minutes.

Add crumbs to the pan along with the celery/onion mixture then add the sherry. Mix with a rubber spatula. Mixture should stick together and form a ball when pressed in the hand. Add a little more sherry and/or butter if it's too dry to stick. Shape into balls each about the size of a large aggie (marble about an inch in diameter) and press each ball into the open cavity of each shrimp, packing well so that there aren't any cracks. Place each shrimp in a pie plate and fold back tail over the stuffing. Add a little water to the pie plate—not on the shrimp—to prevent sticking. Place the pie plate on the middle shelf of the oven for 6-7 minutes. The shrimp should turn pink, and the tails, when pinched, should start to pull away from the shell. Place under the broiler for a minute or two to brown if you wish.

Place in heated dishes and serve with the remaining butter, melted or drawn, on the side, one tablespoon per serving. For additional flavor, put your thumb over the opened top of the sherry bottle and tip up to "spray" sherry over the shrimp as they come from the oven.

Serves 6.

VEGETABLES

SUMMER (Mat-terll-a-waw-kees-wush, Squash ripe, beans edible)

The line between work and play was never more blurred than in summertime. Fishing, serving as Indian guides and picking strawberries, blackberries and blueberries were as much fun as riding our bicycles across dirt roads, swimming and eating blueberry pie. We caddied in Osterville, walking seven or eight miles to the golf course where we'd often carry "doubles" in the morning and "singles" that afternoon before heading back home, hoping someone would pick us up. During these warm months away from school, we were never far from the waters or playing fields.

Our toys were fashioned from scraps. We made our own go-carts, bean snappers, sling shots, hoops and bows out of used rubber inner tubes, leather from discarded shoes, limbs and bushes from the woodlands, shingles and discards at the town dump. We played baseball every chance we got, and many of us graduated to the Cape Cod League. We were outdoors as much as possible.

Summer Activities

Most of our activities, both work and play, were closely related to food. We loved picking grapes and the fruit from our apple, peach and quince trees, in anticipation of the jelly our mother would make. On a hook over the sink she'd hang the cheesecloth bag full of cooked fruit mash and let it drip. She'd tell us not to squeeze the bag because some of the sediment would get in the juice, making the jelly cloudy instead of clear. She'd say, "Don't squeeze that bag, just hang it up and let it drip, drip, drip—right down to the last drop."

When the juice was ready or the fruit mashed up for preserves, our mother would add some pectin as needed, bring the mixture to a rolling boil, add the sugar then bring it back to a boil. It would then be tested for consistency and ladled into heated jars. Our mother allowed us to pour

Left: A bountiful harvest.

Equa Mills, Earl's granddaughter, daughter of "Chiefie" Mills and Carol Lang Mills.

the wax over the jelly and preserves. It was fun to watch the wax envelop the top and eventually turn white. Next the jars would be covered, labeled, dated and put on the shelves in the cellar.

During these warmer months, salespeople came by hawking their wares—selling dry goods, blankets, shellfish, eggs and services such as photography and paintings. They all had their gimmicks for attracting our parents' business. Some would enlist us kids to knock on our own front doors; others would ring a bell, toot a horn, tell stories or perform magic tricks.

The fish man's truck was printed with his slogan, "If it wiggles, we got it." And, of course, if it wiggled, our mother bought it. The fish man gutted and filleted the fish on his tailgate and put the tail, skeleton and head in one bag, which would eventually become our mother's wonderful fish chowder to be enjoyed with fried bread for supper. The fillets would go in another bag; we loved them fried.

Wood cutting time came just before the harvest. We used the wood for heating the house and for cooking, and we sold some. It was fun cutting the wood, partly because we were allowed to use the ax. We'd cut the logs into cords, which was how the wood was sold. The cords would then be picked up by the wood dealer with his horse and wagon. It was a great experience—cutting, measuring, sawing, sharpening the ax with the whetstone and having the feeling of accomplishment along with sharing the experience with our father.

The end of summer is "Wee-pun-na-kees-wush" (corn is edible).

Chen-Ul-Ka Pocknett, Earl's grandson, performing in the
Fancy Dance at the Youth Pow Wow.

The Mashpee Pow Wow

For three days in early July, our world revolves around the annual
Mashpee Pow Wow, which still takes place each year. The Pow Wow
begins with the lighting of the ceremonial fire and cleansing the area with
smoke. Tobacco is placed in the fire as an offering to the Great Spirit
Kiehtan, the Principal Maker of All, then to the spirit world, the ancestors,
the living and the yet unborn.

The Circle Dance at the Mashpee Pow Wow.

Next comes the pipe ceremony, very important because it connects the people with the spiritual world. The pipe is offered stem first to Mother Earth, then to Father Sky, then to the four directions. Finally, the pipe is presented to other tribal representatives. Once all the representatives have smoked the pipe, the ceremony is complete. The host again takes the pipe and presents it to the heavens and says, "We are all related." Festivities can now begin!

The character of the Pow Wow has changed over time. It used to be more spiritual and centered

Very young dancer at the Mashpee Pow Wow.

Earl's grandson, Wamp-Si-Kuk Mills, performing in the Grass Dance at the Youth Pow Wow.

around customs, the fire, orations and ongoing friendships, as well as making new friends. Guest participants stayed in the homes of the members of the host tribe and got to know each other. Today's Pow Wow is a social, spiritual and commercial gathering. Arts, crafts, food, music and dance competitions are integral parts. A modern Pow Wow is more of a festive time—a gathering together of native peoples to reaffirm their heritage, to sing, to conduct dance competitions and to sell and trade ideas and goods.

Songs and dances are forms of oral history that connect Indian people to their past. Over the years, some words of the songs have been changed to allow different tongues to join in the singing.

Dance styles have also changed dramatically. In recent years, Native American dancers have traveled around the country to participate in intertribal dance competitions and to Europe and Russia to perform and to share their rich heritage. As this generation adopts steps and dances from other tribes, customs are blended. This sharing of steps and regalia has led to a better understanding among peoples.

Carrying on the old traditions, each dancer feels and reflects his or her own connection to the spirit of that particular dance, whether it be a bird, animal, fish or some other natural element. If a dancer is truly involved in the dance, he will be at one with the essence of its spirit and the drum, and the judges will sense this interpretation. Regalia represents a crossing over of cultures as dance competitions have introduced the ceremonial

Earl assisting granddaughter Madas Pocknett and grandson Chen-Ul-Ka Pocknett
with regalia for a presentation at the Falmouth Women's Group.

attire of other tribes. Dress is bright, colorful and ornate to attract the attention of the judges.

Pow Wows also feature many traditional dances. Everyone is invited to join in the round dance, a welcome dance for all cultures. In the circle dance, entry into the circle represents order of importance in the society. Folk dances include the calumet, or pipe, dance. Other traditional dances reflecting our heritage and connection to the earth include the fancy dance, fish dance, mat dance, hunters dance, rabbit dance, rattle dance, shawl dance and turtle dance.

Earl Mills Jr. (Chiefie) at the
Mashpee Pow Wow .

Three young friends at the Youth Pow Wow.

Food plays an important role in the Pow Wow, as it does in all of our endeavors, whether work or social. Chowders, steamers, fish stew, soups and smoked herring are mainstays of the event as well as our traditional corn and seafood. I especially look forward to the corn chowder and clams each year. The Pow Wow is a festival of good eating and inviting aromas as well as a celebration of song, dance and reunion.

THE SPIRIT OF MOTHER EARTH

Ohkeannit is a complex Algonkian word that loosely translates as "the
Spirit of Mother Earth." Its prefix is derived from *ohke* meaning "land"
and *ohkas* meaning "mother," both words having the more encompassing
meaning, "producer." The suffix *annit* is literally "the spirit."

The Wampanoag language is derived from Algonkian, the language of
the Algonquian people. They had no written language; their words were
polysynthetic, a combination of many roots and suffixes in a fixed order.
Combining roots and stems allowed for an incalculable number of words
that accurately described and denoted persons, places and things.

The word Ohkeannit, the Spirit of Mother Earth, reflects the homage
given to the Earth Mother, the producer of all basic needs—food, cloth-
ing, shelter and medicine. She is credited with pleasing all of the senses
with her beauty and majesty as well as for providing for her people; her
spirit is to be honored and thanked.

Land and community are the heart and soul of Native American life.
The first responsibility of native people is to preserve and protect the
land, to ensure survival. The earth is the ultimate mother, the most essential member of the community, demanding respect and reverence. This
philosophy includes the necessity to stay level with the rest of creation;
only by staying level can one protect oneself from a fall.

Summer's bounty and Cape Cod home.

Great Spirit, who hast blessed the earth
That it should be fruitful and bring forth
Whatsoever is needful for the life of man,
And has commanded us to work with quietness,
And eat our own bread;
Bless the labors of those who till the fields
And grant such seasonable weather
That we may gather in the fruits of the earth.

General Notes on Vegetables

Consider adding some of the following to your vegetables to perk them up and make them more tempting—almonds, apple juice, applesauce, brown sugar, dried cranberries, garlic, ginger, lemon, light cream, parmesan cheese, pineapple, pine nuts, nutmeg, raisins or white sugar.

Water temperature and cooking methods will depend on your serving plans. You may be serving the vegetables immediately or you may need to have them prepared for a later serving as we do in the restaurant. If starting vegetables in cold water, watch carefully when it starts to boil. Vegetables will continue to cook until they are removed from the heat and the hot water. If you don't plan to serve them immediately, blanch the vegetables then place in ice water and keep cool in the refrigerator. Save some of the cooking water to reheat the vegetables immediately before serving. Large vegetables, such as cauliflower and broccoli, blanch well.

Cut the vegetables carefully, keeping them consistent in size and shape.

— • — • — • — • — • — • — • — • — • — • —

My father could live on beans. When my mother had stewed beans cooking on the back of the old stove, we knew that Johnny cakes or fried bread weren't far behind.

— • — • — • — • — • — • — • — • — • — • —

BAKED BEANS

1 pound beans (pea, kidney or any
   dried bean)
⅓ cup molasses
½ cup brown sugar

1 teaspoon dry mustard
2 level teaspoons salt
¼ teaspoon pepper
½ pound salt pork

Cover beans with water and parboil them in a heavy pot. Cook the beans until they are tender, about 45 minutes to one hour. (This is important because the beans will not get tender while baking.) Do not overcook. Add water as needed.

Add the next five ingredients. Cut the salt pork **just through the rind** to create a grid of small sections.

Add to the beans and bake uncovered at 350°–375° for 6–8 hours. Add water as needed, keeping juice level with the top of the beans (preferably boiling water so cooking won't be retarded).

If you prefer that the beans stay light on the top, keep the pot covered during the cooking time. I prefer the beans nicely browned on top, so I remove the cover during the last hour of cooking.

Serves 8–12.

BEETS

Buy beets with the tops still attached. Wash thoroughly in plenty of cold water. Cut off and set aside greens.

Place beets in cold water with salt to taste. Cook until tender. Remove beets and strain, reserving the water, and allow to cool. Peel with a knife or rub with your hands to remove the outer covering.

Cut the greens across the stems in 1–2-inch lengths. Return the greens to the beet water and cook until tender.

Slice and add the beets, salt and pepper to taste, and butter as desired. Bring to a simmer.

PICKLED BEETS

2 beets with greens   ½ cup sugar
½ cup vinegar   5 slices small red onion

Cook beets as directed above. Using slightly more vinegar than sugar, mix the sugar and vinegar with some of the beet water until the sugar is dissolved.

Add onions and sliced beets to the sugar/vinegar mixture. Let marinate in the refrigerator for an hour or longer before serving.

Serves 2.

HARVARD BEETS

Either slice the beets or use tiny ones. Mix the sugar and vinegar as directed above. Combine equal amounts (about 1 tablespoon) of cornstarch and water and add to the beet juice to thicken it. Add butter, salt and pepper to taste.

CABBAGE

½ head cabbage, shredded
2 tablespoons melted butter

½ cup Parmesan cheese
1 cup light cream

Preheat oven to 375°.

Bring salted water to a boil and add cabbage. Bring water back to a boil and blanch cabbage for 30 seconds. Drain thoroughly.

Place cabbage in a pie plate or on a small baking dish. Press down firmly, making sure that cabbage isn't too wet. Add butter, Parmesan cheese, and cream. Bake until bubbling and brown.

An optional method is to sauté cooked cabbage with butter, salt and pepper. Add Parmesan cheese at the table.

Serves 6.

RED CABBAGE

This is a great vegetable with boiled meats!

1 small red cabbage
¼ cup brown sugar
approximately ⅛ cup vinegar

approximately ½ cup apple sauce
Dash nutmeg

Shred one small cabbage. Add to boiling, salted water. Blanch and drain cabbage thoroughly then return to pan. Add remaining ingredients. Heat thoroughly.

Serves 6.

CARROTS

Cut carrots so that they are consistent in size and shape. (I prefer the Chinese cut—roll the carrot and slice on an angle.) Barely cover the carrots with boiling water. Add salt and sugar to the water and cook to desired tenderness. You may finish the carrots in any of several ways. Additional ingredients such as brown sugar should be used according to personal preference.

For glazed carrots, undercook carrots. Add brown sugar, butter and lemon and sauté. Use a little of the carrot water or maple syrup to glaze. For creamed carrots, add cooked carrots to cream sauce.

If you wish nutmeg carrots, butter cooked carrots and add a sprinkle of nutmeg. Another tasty way to serve this vegetable is parslied carrots— chop up parsley and add with butter to cooked carrots.

JAG

1 medium onion, chopped
6 tablespoons oil
  OR ½ stick margarine and 2
  tablespoons oil
2 cups frozen lima beans

2¼ cups water
1½ cups long grain rice
1½ teaspoons salt
¼ teaspoon pepper

Sauté onion in oil. Add lima beans and sauté for 1–2 minutes. Add water, rice, salt and pepper. Cover and bring to a slow simmer. Turn heat down. Cook until rice is done.

When lima beans come to the top, fold them back into the rice with a spatula or a wooden spoon.

Jag should be dry.

POTATO BARGAIN
"Force Me Down" Poor Man's Scalloped Potatoes

⅛ pound salt pork, cut in bite size
  pieces through the rind and
  rendered*
1 medium onion, sliced
4 medium potatoes, sliced thin
¼ teaspoon black pepper

1½ teaspoons salt
optional: ¼ teaspoon curry powder,
  4 hot dogs
  Olive oil or margarine may be substituted for the salt pork.

"Bargain" should be done on top of the stove in a cast iron (spider) pan with a cover.

Render pork, pouring off excess fat and leaving pork scraps in pan. Sauté onion in pork fat until well browned.

Slice potatoes crosswise. Separate the potato slices as you place them in the pan; otherwise the starch and water may cause them to stick together. Add salt, pepper and enough water to cover the potatoes. Cover and let simmer until the potatoes are tender.

You can dress up the dish by adding curry powder near the end of the cooking time. Mix the curry powder in a dish with some of the "bargain" gravy to dissolve. Add as many hot dogs as desired. *If you've made too much, give me a call!*

Serves 4–6.

ACORN SQUASH

2 acorn squashes   ¼ cup butter or margarine
6 tablespoons brown sugar   ¾ teaspoon nutmeg
¼ cup maple syrup   ¼–½ teaspoon salt

Preheat oven to 375°.

Cut squash in half and/or quarters (depending on size) and remove the pulp and seeds.

Place in a medium-size baking dish, skin side down. Cover bottom with water. Mix and add the remaining ingredients to the squash cavity.

Cover dish with foil. Bake for 40 minutes, basting two to three times during cooking.

Serves 6.

Every day diners ask for my squash recipe. That's a hard order. Not because there's any secret; it's just that it's easy as long as you taste as you go. The secret is in not letting the squash overcook and in finding the perfect balance between the flavors of the vegetable, the salt and the brown sugar.

The more surface you have, the more water your food will absorb. Therefore, I suggest cutting the squash in large chunks to keep it from becoming mushy. Do not overcook. It should be firm, but not hard.

BUTTERNUT SQUASH

1 large butternut squash
2–3 teaspoons salt (depending on squash—just enough to bring out flavor)
½ teaspoon white pepper
¼–½ cup butter and/or margarine
¼–½ cup brown sugar

Peel, seed and cut squash into 2-inch chunks. Add to boiling water and simmer for about 15 minutes, just until it is fork tender.

Remove from heat, strain well and whip until smooth. Add salt, pepper and butter. Taste test before adding brown sugar. Add brown sugar in small increments, tasting as you go. Brown sugar should balance out the raw squash flavor.

Serves 6.

BROILED TOMATO

One whole small tomato or ½ large tomato per person
Sugar, salt and butter for topping, as needed
Bread crumbs for topping, as needed
Parmesan cheese for topping, as needed

Preheat the oven to 375°.

Remove the top of the tomato, pierce it with a fork and top with sprinkled sugar, salt and a dab of butter. Place the tomato in a broiler pan in a little water. Broil until it starts to bubble.

Top the tomato with bread crumbs and Parmesan cheese and bake until lightly browned. Delicious with Welsh Rarebit (*see* recipe on page 31.) and a slice of bacon.

Original oil painting by Dr. Walton C. Galinat showing a Native American holding *teosinte* as it was first discovered and corn as we know it today. This painting was presented to Earl Mills through Betty Breen and now hangs in The Flume restaurant, Mashpee, Massachusetts, on Cape Cod. Photo used with permission.

CORN

Research by Dr. Walton C. Galinat

> *The American Indians were not simply the first corn breeders.*
> *They created corn in the first place.*
>   Dr. Walton C. Galinat

One of the nicest things about doing this book has been meeting people who have become friends as well as valued authorities on subjects we were researching. Much of the world views Dr. Walton C. Galinat as we do. He is a distinguished economic botanist, poet, artist, teacher, writer and lecturer as well as a charming and friendly man with a quirky sense of humor.

    Dr. Galinat's association with corn, the plant known as *zea maize*, dates back to his high school days. His early work on the genetics of the plant was the prelude to a lifelong association with corn.

Regular and ornamental ears of corn.

In his 60 years of research and study at the Bussey Institute at Harvard University and at the Waltham Field Station (associated with the University of Massachusetts), Dr. Galinat has worked in agronomy, genetics, research and education. He has shared his wealth of knowledge with us, with his students and with scientists in the classroom and laboratory. His papers have appeared in over 300 publications and have been delivered worldwide. His current laboratory at the Waltham Field Station is a veritable museum to corn and a sanctuary for his books, seeds, plants, drawings, poems and copious notes.

"Corn is my religion, and this laboratory is my church," he claims. However, it is apparent that humanity rules his heart and soul. In his paper *Corn, Columbus and Culture,* distributed by the University of Chicago in 1992, Dr. Galinat writes:

> In the future, as population pressure and our understanding of maize both increase, this crop's role as our symbiotic partner in survival will also increase. As the most intelligent species on the only planet known to contain life, it behooves us to use our intelligence not only to harmonize our symbiotic relationship with plants but also with each other and especially with other races or minorities or people so that tribal warfare is forgotten.

We are grateful to Dr. Galinat for the use of his many research papers, his painting and his knowledge. Most of all, we appreciate the gift of his time.

Corn—Zea Maize

No one knows when corn, or *maize*, first appeared in New England. In spite of its cloudy history, researchers generally agree that corn as we know it today originated in the Americas some tens of thousands of years ago. By the time the plant reached northern Indians, cultivation had resulted in a plant unable to reproduce by itself, dependent on man for reseeding.

Subject to the whims of nature and climate and with only animal bones, shells, stones and wood for tools, Indians in the north had planted corn in little mounds. They fertilized the plants with fish heads gathered during the spring spawning runs, when thousands of herring and alewives were trapped during the upstream migration.

Myles Standish reported that Pilgrims arriving on the beach along the Pamet River in Truro on Cape Cod spotted mounds of sand that aroused their curiosity. Investigation uncovered a cache of seed corn buried under the sand. The settlers raided the mounds and returned some ten days later to help themselves once again to the fruits of Indian toil and storage. A stone on Corn Hill in Truro reads:

> Sixteen Pilgrims led by
> Myles Standish, William Bradford,
> Stephen Hopkins and Edward Tilley
> found this precious Indian corn
> on this spot which they called Corn Hill.
> And sure it was God's good providence
> that we found this corn else
> we know not how we should have done.

Maize sustained the English settlers in Plymouth Colony when their crops of wheat, barley and peas failed during their first summer. In the spring of 1621, an Indian named Squanto taught the English settlers how to plant grains of corn in little hills four feet apart. Squanto had been captured, sold into slavery, sent to Spain and then to England where he learned to speak English. His lessons in planting and fertilizing assured the survival of those newcomers who hadn't succumbed to their first New England winter.

Maize had become so vital to the settlers that Captain John Smith decreed that every family in the Virginia colony grow corn. On October 8, 1631, maize was made legal tender in Massachusetts Bay Colony for all

Earl's granddaughter, Madas Pocknett,
with ears of corn.

transactions, unless pelts of fur were specified in the agreement. Corn has been called the "kernel of civilization," "the milk of the land," and "the grain that built a civilization."

To the Indians, corn was food for the gods and man, a gift from the Great Spirit. Aside from making corn a staple of their diet, Native Americans found uses for every part of the plant. Husks filled mattresses; they were also braided into mats, trays, baskets, rugs and sleeping pads or used to make moccasins. Dried husks started fires. Stalks were made into fences and hollowed out for use as medicine bottles. Dolls were made from cobs.

The women and children of the tribe gathered corn. Husking was a festive community activity. The fresh corn was sometimes cut from the cob and boiled as soup with beans and berries. Kernels were fried in oil; corn meal was shaped into dumplings and cooked with meat or boiled with pumpkin and maple sugar. The Indians roasted sweet ears of green corn inside their inner husks in ashes under a shallow layer of earth and hot coals. Green corn was parched, cooked until light brown, coated with animal fat and eaten on the cob.

Although highly valued by the Indians, early use of the plant represented only a fraction of its potential. Today only three percent of all corn grown comes to our common table as the all-American favorite, corn on the cob; the remainder is used for fodder or finds its way into every room in our homes in one product or other. Modern technology has turned corn and its plant into over 2,000 products essential to our lives today. Far more than a major food source; corn is the basis of our supply of meat, milk and eggs. It is the most important crop in the Western Hemisphere and exceeded in value worldwide only by wheat and rice.

In the Americas where maize originated, it is called corn. In all other parts of the world except Britain and Australia it is known as maize.

Beans, corn and squash are known by native people as the "Three Sisters." They are grown beside each other, even staked and tied together, because of their symbiotic effect. Beans provide nitrogen and nourishment to the soil. Corn provides a trellis for climbing beans, as well as shade and condensation of water. Squash creates ground cover to suppress the weeds and protect from insects. Together they provide a balanced diet and remind us of the interdependence of all of Kiehtan's creations.

Promise of a successful harvest.

In the place where we live,
Tobacco, corn and other gifts grow.
They have been given to us to act
As a communication between
The two-leggeds and the Great Mystery.
We give thanksgiving to these beings
Who aid our communication
With the Great Mystery.

CORN

Corn is easy and quick to prepare. To cook frozen corn, add to boiling salted water. Add sugar to taste and bring back to a simmer. For creamed corn, add light cream, butter and salt and pepper to taste.

In cooking corn on the cob, barely cover corn with cold water. Add 1 tablespoon of sugar. Bring to a boil and cook for 5 minutes. If corn sits in water, the water will remove its sweetness. Milk will add sweetness, so if corn is to be held for a later serving, add one cup of milk to the water. (If you're trying to eliminate or reduce the butter in your diet, adding milk to the water may be a sufficient replacement for the butter.)

CORN CHOWDER

You may use cream-style corn, corn niblets and/or corn cut off the cob for this chowder. If you cut the corn from the cob, cook the cobs in with the potatoes for added flavor.

4 teaspoons salt	4 cups chicken stock
3–4 potatoes, diced	4 cups corn
2 medium onions, chopped	3 cups milk, whole or skimmed
2 tablespoons olive oil, butter or margarine	OR 2 cans evaporated milk
4 tablespoons butter or margarine	1 teaspoon black pepper
4 tablespoons flour	1 green pepper, seeded and sliced

Place potatoes and 2 teaspoons of salt in a saucepan with enough water to barely cover the potatoes. Simmer until tender. Don't strain the water. Set aside.

Sauté onions in 2 tablespoons of olive oil, butter or margarine. Cook until soft. Add to the potatoes and water.

Melt the remaining 4 tablespoons of butter or margarine in a large saucepan. Add flour and stir over medium heat until mixture (roux) reaches the consistency of corn meal. Add the chicken stock and the water from potatoes. Cook until thickened, whipping continually. Add the corn and the milk.

Gradually add the potatoes and onions to the thickened mixture. Continue to simmer and add the additional 2 teaspoons of salt (to taste) along with the sliced green pepper. Simmer for 2–3 minutes. Add fresh ground pepper to taste now or when serving.

Serves 10–12.

FERDINAND MILLS' CORN BREAD

2 cups stone ground corn meal
½ cup flour
⅜ cup sugar
1 teaspoon salt

3 teaspoons baking powder
1 egg
1 cup milk

Preheat oven to 425° and butter an 8 x 8-inch baking pan.

Measure the dry ingredients into a bowl and give them a couple of turns with a whisk to mix.

In another bowl, add the egg and milk, whisking just to blend. Add the dry ingredients all at once and fold in just to moisten.

Scrape into the baking pan with a rubber spatula. Bake for 20 minutes or until corn bread pulls away from the sides of the pan.

Serves 6.

Bunny Lopez, Chief Silent Drum, Mashpee
Wampanoags, at the Mashpee Pow Wow.

━ ▪ ━ ▪ ━ ▪ ━ ▪ ━ ▪ ━ ▪ ━ ▪ ━ ▪ ━ ▪ ━

Johnny cake is a modern name for an Indian food made from corn meal and water or milk. A little salt, sugar or fat may have been added, if available. The mixture was baked flat over an open fire and probably carried and eaten during journeys or hunting expeditions. Its name is most likely derived from the term journey cake.

━ ▪ ━ ▪ ━ ▪ ━ ▪ ━ ▪ ━ ▪ ━ ▪ ━ ▪ ━ ▪ ━

JOHNNY CAKES

My father used the above recipe for his corn cakes and Johnny cakes. He simply added ¼–½ cup of milk to the batter, heated a spider or heavy frying pan, added butter and/or bacon fat and spooned the batter by tablespoons into the pan to make the little cakes. It's necessary to control the heat to keep the cakes from burning. Keep a platter warm in the oven until all the batter is used. Place cakes on the heated platter. These cakes are a great accompaniment to stewed beans, Potato Bargain or stews.

— . — . — . — . — . — . — . — . — . —

Corn bread, or pone, is derived from the Algonkian word *apan* which means "baked." Small loaves of corn bread wrapped in corn husks and baked over hot ashes were known as ash cakes. Hoecakes were small loaves of corn bread molded over hoes and baked over an open fire.

— . — . — . — . — . — . — . — . — . —

CORN BREAD
(White Corn Cake)

½ cup stone ground corn meal
½ cup all-purpose unbleached flour
1 teaspoon cream of tartar
½ teaspoon baking soda
¼ teaspoon salt

2 tablespoons butter, softened
2 tablespoons granulated sugar
1 large egg
½ cup milk

Preheat oven to 425° and grease a loaf pan.

Measure the corn meal, flour, cream of tartar, baking soda and salt into a bowl and give them a couple of turns with a whisk to mix and break up any lumps. In another bowl, cream the softened butter with the sugar. Separate the egg. Stir in the egg yolk, and beat the egg white into soft peaks. Add the milk to the butter/sugar/yolk mixture. Give it a stir or two. Do not blend until smooth. Add the dry ingredients all at once and stir just enough to moisten. **Do not overmix!** Fold in the beaten egg white. Scrape into the loaf pan with a rubber spatula.

Bake for 20 minutes, or until the sides have pulled away from the pan. This corn bread is worth the extra effort! If you wish, you can double the recipe and use an 8 x 8 x 2-inch pan.

Serves 4–6.

CORN SPOON BREAD
(from George and Barbara Bush)

The following quote from the office of George Bush accompanied this recipe: "President and Mrs. Bush have many favorite dishes, but the enclosed recipe is one of the family's most popular. The Bushes are pleased to submit this for your cookbook project, and they send their best wishes for success with your effort."

1 can creamed corn	3 eggs
1 cup yellow corn meal	1 teaspoon salt
¾ cup milk	4 ounces chopped green chilies
⅓ cup oil	1 cup grated cheese

Mix together and bake in a 375° oven for 25–30 minutes. If you double the recipe, cook for 30–45 minutes.

Serves 6.

The corn Columbus brought back to Europe wasn't immediately accepted. By 1525, corn was growing in southern Spain, and eventually the plant found its way into Italy where polenta became a staple in the diet. Portuguese people brought corn into grain-poor Africa where the plant grew quickly and was often the only source of food. Slaves being carried to the New World often lived on a diet of nothing more than corn meal and water. The ships carrying them brought Indian corn full circle back to America.

JALAPEÑO & CHEDDAR CORN BREAD

1 cup milk
½ teaspoon to 1 tablespoon sugar
1 tablespoon baking powder
1 cup flour
1 cup corn meal
½ teaspoon salt*
1 tablespoon cheddar cheese

2 tablespoons Jalapeño peppers
2 tablespoons corn
2 tablespoons onions
1 tablespoon bacon fat
If substituting bacon drippings with another shortening or eliminating the cheese, you can use a little more salt.

Preheat oven to 400°. Coat an 8 x 8-inch pan with bacon drippings.

Heat milk to just warm. Combine all remaining ingredients. Add milk a little at a time; batter should not seem too moist. Add a little more or less milk if necessary.

Bake for 20-25 minutes.

Serves 6.

Billy Red Dove Mills at the Youth Pow Wow.

Eaten with herring, the roughage of the dumplings pre-
vents any small bones that may remain in the fish from
becoming lodged in the throat. Dumplings, when
added to soups or stews, are smaller—the Native
American equivalent of matzoh balls. They are
dropped from a teaspoon into the broth and simmered for five minutes.

CORN MEAL DUMPLINGS
(from Cora DeGrasse Whiting)

2 cups corn meal
1 cup boiling water
½ cup flour

1½ teaspoons baking powder
1 teaspoon salt

Scald the corn meal with boiling water. Let cool.

Add the flour, baking powder and salt. Shape into a serving spoon and
drop into simmering water or stock for 8–12 minutes.

Serves 6.

— · — · — · — · — · — · — · — · — · —

The different pigments of corn are literally only skin deep, the pigment being limited to a thin layer covering the endosperm just inside the outer layer of the hull. The corn we hang on our doors in the fall and call Indian Corn is misnamed. It is ornamental corn. All corn is Indian Corn.

— · — · — · — · — · — · — · — · — · —

MASHPEE SPIDER CORN CAKE

1⅓ cups stone ground corn meal
⅓ cup flour*
¾ teaspoon baking soda
¾ teaspoon cream of tartar
¼ cup sugar
½ teaspoon salt
1 large egg, well beaten

1 cup sour milk
½ cup milk
1½ tablespoons butter
1 cup milk
*Option: whole wheat flour
Tip: Serve with more butter or
    mapel syrup, or both on top.

Preheat oven to 375°.

Measure the dry ingredients in a bowl and give them a couple of turns with a whisk to mix thoroughly and break up any lumps. In a separate bowl, whisk the egg gently. Add the sour milk and ½ cup of milk, whisking to blend.

Five minutes before you are ready to bake the corn cake, put the butter into a heavy, oven-proof skillet (black spider) and place in the hot oven.

Add the egg and milk mixture to the dry ingredients and whisk, just enough to blend. After the skillet has been in the oven for 5 minutes, remove it and thoroughly coat it with the now-melted butter by carefully swirling the butter around the bottom and up the sides. Pour any excess butter into the batter and scrape the batter into the still hot skillet with a rubber spatula. Dribble the remaining ½ cup of milk over the surface of the batter. Return the skillet to the oven and bake the corn cake for approximately 50 minutes, or until set and nicely browned.

Remove from the oven and invert the cake onto a cutting board. Serve in wedges with browned side up. Prick with a fork to allow the butter or maple syrup to soak in. Note the delicate line of custard!

Serves 6.

SUCCOTASH

3 ears of corn with cobs
   OR 3–4 cups canned niblets
1 medium onion, minced
4 stalks celery, chopped fine
3 tablespoons butter

3–4 cups chicken stock, chicken
   broth or water
2 cups frozen lima beans
Salt and pepper to taste

If using corn on the cob, remove the kernels from the cobs.

In a large saucepan, sauté the celery and onion in 3 tablespoons butter. Add the cobs to the sautéed celery and onions.

Add chicken stock, broth or water and let simmer for 5 minutes. Add the lima beans and let simmer until the beans are tender. If using the corn off the cob, add with the lima beans. If using canned corn, add just before the lima beans are done.

You may want to add a pinch of sugar if using canned corn. Remove cobs before serving.

Six 6.

David Pocknett announcing at the Youth Pow Wow.

CRANBERRIES

FALL (Poh-quit-a-qunk,
The middle between summer and winter)

If it's true that everything has a season, then it seems to me that Cape Cod is most comfortable with itself in late fall. Fields lie fallow, harvested bogs and gardens are at rest, and seasonal residents and wildlife are preparing to head south. The land is at peace with itself; it's time to give thanks.

Living by the seasons required planning. While we were busy with current projects, we were getting ready for the next cycle. Picking cranberries was next on the agenda. It was time to get out the knee pads, check the scoops, wipe mineral oil on the teeth of the rocker scoops and repair the snap scoops. All harvests were festive times, but cranberry season was particularly exciting because men would take their vacations to return to Mashpee for the harvest; the money was good and it was a reunion of sorts with lots of good food.

Meanwhile, scallop season was approaching and it'd be time to get the scallop "glass," nets and bull rakes out. The glass was really a box with glass on the bottom, something like a miniature glass bottom boat. The scalloper would let the boat drift, using the side of the boat as the fulcrum with the glass over the side and a long-handled net in the other hand. Looking through the glass, he could see the outline of a scallop in the mud. The scalloper would move the net around to scoop the scallops up and empty the net into the boat. He kept track of where he was by watching the horizon.

Some of the really good scallopers were Nathan Peters, Edwin White, my father, Milteer Hendricks, Carl Avant and Nathan Peters Jr., whom we called "Pop." Mr. White had a spot under his house like a little garage area where he'd shuck his scallops. Mr. Peters had a shed with a lamp hanging from the rafters over the scallop table. After suppertime, we'd take our knives and go to the selected fisherman's home where we would open

Wet cranberry bog showing a flume, a dam used to raise and lower the water in the bogs. The Flume restaurant gets its name from this device.

scallops and be paid by the quart. They had cans—I think 5 gallon cans—with pressure tight tops into which the opened scallops would be poured.

Opening the scallops was a communal time for sitting, talking and camaraderie. Once in a while, a scallop would accidentally flip into my mouth, especially if it had a little pink color. I want to tell you that's some good eatin'. I knew I'd better not start doing that because soon I'd be eating a few more than I was opening. The opening of scallops was not all fun and games. By the end of the night, my hands would be sore from the nicks and cuts received from the knife and the sharp edges of the shells.

The scallop man came by every night in his old truck. At each stop, he'd hook the scale to the bracket on the side of the truck, weigh the fisherman's catch and give him the day's market price. There was a ten-bushel limit and practically everyone got his limit.

Scallop glasses and nets were fine for personal use, but bull rakes were used for gathering ten bushels. The bull rake had a big wire basket on its top side. We'd throw the rake overboard and pull it towards the boat to get the scallops from the bottom of the bay into the wire basket. Using the side of the boat, the basket was turned over and mud shaken out as it was drawn to the boat. The scallops were then taken out, put in the bottom of the boat and the process repeated. Hard work!

Then it was time to get ready to go eeling. We'd get the eel spears out, making sure each spear was firmly attached to its handle. Now many eelers use traps, and that's part of the reason we can't find many eels; eelers with traps just take everything regardless of size.

With the eel spear, we could only catch a certain size because we'd have to feel in the mud for them and thrust the spear back and forth. Sometimes we'd have three or four eels on that spear in between those hooks, and we'd bring that up and have our hands full. There'd be enough eels on the bottom on that spear to provide supper for the whole family. The eels were in the bottom of the boat so we had to be careful we didn't fall overboard because they'd be squirming around.

Eels were generally served with boiled "taters," rendered salt pork fat for moisture and some summer squash. Crispy salt pork pieces were served on the side. I loved eels, and just thinking about how many skeletons I had next to my plate conjures up memories of some good eating,

Before supper was finished, my mom would get up and whip up a simple dessert that would be ready by the time we were done eating. Maybe it would be boiled rice with whipped eggs, sugar and vanilla poured over it. Or maybe a hot custard made in the twinkling of an eye. Sometimes she'd whip up a hot milk cake. When the cake was ready to come out, she'd whip up some cream with a little sugar in it and vanilla or lemon extract and put a dollop of cream over it. I want to tell you, boy, that was some, some, some good eating.

We always had people stopping in at suppertime. She'd just set another place. My parents were good providers and very good cooks. In my memories, we were rich. We had all kinds of things and all kinds of foods.

A variety of scallop shells. The larger shells are from sea scallops; the smaller ones with more ridges are native, or cape, scallops and oh so sweet!.

Water harvesting.

We thank you, O Mysterious One
For providing for those who are hungry.
Gather us all together to share this food
And give thanks for your bounty.

CRANBERRIES (Sassamenesh)

People "from away" quickly notice that cranberry bogs are as much a part of the landscape of Cape Cod as salt marshes and sand dunes. Sometimes the bogs are green; at other times they're a magnificent burgundy. They may be flooded or dry. Most visitors don't give the berries much thought until they appear on their Thanksgiving tables.

English settlers dubbed the plant the "crane-berry" after the white blossoms that appear in early June resembling the heads of cranes. Native Americans had long valued the berry known to them as the "Sassamenesh." Like its name, the cranberry has continually adapted to modernization and change. In many ways, the history of this indigenous fruit mirrors that of the native people.

Along about the beginning of September, when the sky darkened slightly and there was a snap in the evening air, people in Mashpee would begin to think about harvesting cranberries. In the early days, school opened later in the year to allow the children to do the hand picking. Later on, they could be excused from school to pick cranberries by the measureful under the direction of some of the tribal group's elder women, who would supervise the kids as well as pick by hand themselves.

Miss Tina Pocknett Sturgis was one of those women and one of the best hand pickers I ever saw. She was very fragile and feminine, and she'd just walk along with kind of a spring in her step and jump across a ditch. This always amazed us kids, because we'd have to run halfway across the bog to clear the same ditch.

The old bogs had several ditches. A marginal ditch went around the whole periphery of the bog to keep it free from briars and encroaching ground covers. Additional ditches emanated from that outer ditch and provided moisture, which created a mist on cold nights and helped to protect the berries from freezing. Modern irrigation methods have since replaced all but the marginal ditch, leaving more space to grow the berries.

Before modernization, harvesting was a festive time. My uncles and cousins would take time off from their jobs to work on the bogs. Although the work was back breaking, the money they made on the bogs was probably two or three times more than they made on their regular jobs. Relatives who had moved away often came back to the town for the harvest, and there was a sense of community with everyone working together. My mother and grandmother prepared favorite old dishes for the uncles and aunts who would be coming and staying with relatives.

The morning of the first picking we'd head to the bogs with our brown bags. We'd arrive around 9 or 9:30 because we couldn't get on the bog until it dried out. If it had been damp or if the dew was still hanging around on the bogs, we'd have to wait longer for the sand to dry out a little bit. On rainy days we wouldn't go to the bog at all.

We would go at it until about 3:30 or so, no later than four o'clock, because the man who was wheeling the berries off the bog had to get them off before dark to get them to the places where they would be screened. The berries would be all lined up behind each of the pickers waiting for a *wheeler*. A wheeler was a worker who gathered the day's harvest with an extended wheelbarrow. The best wheelers I remember were Winslow "Biffa" Newcomb and Arnold "Dint" Newcomb. They had big arms, great big forearms. They'd have 8–10 boxes loaded on big wheelbarrows and sometimes, when they'd hit the planks at the beginning of the ditches, those berries would pop right up in the boxes.

The Gifford brothers had a screening house with a conveyor belt where the elder women in the community sorted the berries. The berries dropped down onto the belt and bounced into a little box if they were hard and firm. The women would remove the sticks and vines. Berries that didn't bounce went into a separate box, which was emptied outside. For years people used the vines and discarded berries for mulching their gardens.

With dry harvesting, the berries were never in the water; therefore, the entire crop could either be sold locally or shipped to market. Most of the berries were delivered to Wareham or to the Plymouth and Carver areas. Ocean Spray was then, as it is today, the big cooperative.

Berries that will go to market to be sold fresh or frozen are still dry harvested using modern methods. Motorized scoops are used to comb the berries off the vines. Instead of being wheeled off the bogs, a helicopter hooks onto containers holding between 50 and 75 bushels and takes the crates to screening houses where they're processed. The entire operation is mechanized. One helicopter does what it took several men like "Dint" and "Biffa'" weeks to do, and it does it in one fell swoop

Today, ninety percent of all Massachusetts-grown cranberries are wet harvested. Since wet berries aren't marketable as fresh or frozen products, they are used for juice, jellies and other cranberry products. Water picking is cleaner and more successful.

Before a wet harvesting, the bog is flooded. Flat-tired vehicles called reels or "eggbeaters" are driven through the bog, separating the berries from the plants. Once the berries float to the top of the water, they're gathered into hinged planks fashioned into corrals to contain the berries. A huge flexible pipe like a vacuum tube runs from a nearby truck beneath the corral. Berries and water are vacuumed into the tube and carried into the back of the truck, where the vines are separated from the berries.

Each year the season was heralded by the arrival of bog owners on our doorsteps asking who'd be available for picking. Back when I was just about twelve years old, Mr. Maynard Gifford from Cotuit came inquiring about workers. He had a little curved pipe, and he worked out of a small bog house on a knoll in the middle of the bogs. The bogs were owned by his brother, Congressman Charles Gifford, over on Santuit Pond at Bryant's Neck, an area named for Solomon Bryant, one of our Indian preachers at the Old Meeting House.

In later years, Mr. Bertram Ryder would come by in his wooden-bodied beach wagon, putt-putting into the yard with a hand-rolled cigarette hanging from his lip and say to my father, "Well, Ferdinand, yup, it's almost that time. Guess we're gonna have a good crop this yee-ah." Then they'd talk about cranberry business, about what they'd done all summer and about whether or not the season would be a good one.

Earl's granddaughter, Madas Pocknett, with cranberries.

CRANBERRY SAUCE (JELLY)

4 cups cranberries
2 cups water

2 cups cranberry juice (from cooking)
1 cup sugar

Pick over and wash berries. Place berries in a 2-quart saucepan with 2 cups of water. Cook until tender and strain through a double layer of wet cheesecloth. Measure 2 cups of juice and add with sugar to the saucepan.

Bring to a rolling boil, continually stirring, and continue to boil for one minute. Pour into container.

Serves 12–16.

CRANBERRY SAUCE (WHOLE BERRY)

2 cups cranberries
1 cup water

1 cup sugar

Pick over and wash berries. In a 2-quart saucepan, add berries with 1 cup of water and cook until tender.

Add sugar and cook 3-5 minutes longer or to a rolling boil.

Serves 12–16.

CRANBERRY CHUTNEY
(Thanks to Charlie Cremens)

2 Granny Smith apples
2 oranges
4 cups cranberries
1 cup sliced onions
1 cup water
¾ cup dark brown sugar
½ cup granulated sugar

¾ cup cider vinegar
½ teaspoon salt
1 teaspoon grated ginger
½ teaspoon mace
½ teaspoon curry powder
½ cup small black raisins

Peel and dice apples. Grate rind of both oranges, creating zest. Squeeze juice from oranges. Check cranberries and wash.

Simmer the onions, water and the sugars for 30 minutes. Stir in the vinegar, apples, seasonings and orange zest. Boil slowly for another 30 minutes.

Stir in the orange juice, cranberries and raisins. Simmer for another 10 minutes, or until the cranberries burst.

Makes about one quart.

The snap scoop got its name because of the sound it made. Elwood was a really good snap scooper because he could use both hands; he'd rest his right hand for a while and scoop a little with his left hand. There was a rhythm to the way he'd open up the snap scoop and push it into the vine and then snap it shut … snappa … into the vines and pull away, into the vines and pull away. Then he'd take his hand and go up and down the metal spokes of the snap scoop, take the vines out and then pour the beautiful ruby red or off-white berries into a box, generally a half-bushel box.

Some of the other snap scoopers were Teddy Jonas and his father, Mr. Tom "Pepper" Jonas, who could really handle that snap scoop. Merwin Sturgis was another good snap scooper; very clean and thorough. He didn't leave too many berries on the bottom of the bog; he did a nice job. Richardson Jonas and I could pick okay, but we really weren't snap scoopers as such.

SENATOR JOHN F. KERRY'S CRANBERRY BREAD

¼ cup butter or margarine,
    softened
1 cup sugar
2 eggs
1 cup chopped cranberries
½ cup water
½ teaspoon vanilla

1¾ cups flour
½ teaspoon baking soda
½ teaspoon baking powder
1 teaspoon salt
½ teaspoon cinnamon
½ cup chopped walnuts

Preheat oven to 325°. Grease and flour an 8 x 4 x 4-inch loaf pan.

Cream the butter or margarine and sugar together in a large mixing bowl. Beat in eggs with an electric mixer. Stir in cranberries, water and vanilla.

Sift the flour, baking soda, baking powder, salt and cinnamon together, and stir in with the batter. Add chopped nuts to the mixture, then pour into the pan.

Bake for 55 minutes. Test with a toothpick.

Serves 8.

CRANBERRY COFFEE CAKE

½ cup margarine
1 cup sugar
2 eggs, beaten
2 cups flour
1 teaspoon baking powder
½ teaspoon baking soda
1 cup sour cream
1teaspoon almond flavoring

1 16-ounce can whole berry
   cranberry sauce

Glaze
¾ cup confectioner's sugar
½ teaspoon almond flavoring
2 tablespoons warm water

Preheat oven to 350°. Grease and flour a Bundt pan.

Cream margarine and sugar. Add beaten eggs and beat again. Sift dry ingredients together. Mix the sour cream and almond flavoring together.

Alternate adding the flour mixture and the sour cream mixture to the creamed mixture. Spread half of the batter in the cake pan. Add the cranberry sauce and top with the remaining batter. Bake for 55 minutes.

Mix together ingredients for the glaze and pour over warm cake.

Serves 8.

CRANBERRY NUT BREAD

2 cups all-purpose flour
½ teaspoon baking soda
½ teaspoon salt
8 tablespoons butter, melted
  (one stick)
1 cup sugar
2 eggs

1 orange
buttermilk
1 cup chopped walnuts or pecans
1 cup chopped cranberries
  (fresh or dried)

Preheat oven to 350°. Grease a loaf pan with butter, margarine or spray.

Whisk together the flour, baking soda and salt. In a separate bowl, beat the butter, sugar and eggs for two minutes. Grate the orange and save the rind. Juice the orange into a measuring cup.

Add enough buttermilk to the orange juice to equal 1 cup of liquid. Add the grated orange rind to the buttermilk and stir into the egg mixture. Fold in the flour mixture. Dust the chopped cranberries with flour to prevent them from sinking in the batter. Gently fold in the cranberries and nuts.

Bake for 50-60 minutes.

Serves 8.

CAPE COD CRANBERRY SCONES
(from Ann Macdonald-Dailey, The Tea Shoppe, Mashpee Commons)

Ann's Grandmother Mulligan's traditional Irish scones were adapted by Virginia Spargo Macdonald during summer vacations at "Old Maushop" Village on Popponesset Beach using local Cape Cod cranberries. They are served with tea, clotted cream and jam.

4 cups all-purpose flour
⅜ cup sugar
2 tablespoons baking powder
½ pound cold unsalted butter
4 eggs

1 cup heavy cream
1 tablespoon vanilla
1½ cups chopped cranberries
optional: ½ cup chopped walnuts

Preheat oven to 350°.

Combine flour, sugar, and baking powder. Cut in butter until mixture resembles corn meal. In a separate bowl mix the eggs, cream and vanilla. Mix with dry ingredients until just moistened. Add the cranberries and, if desired, the walnuts.

Drop by ⅓ cup or by 3-ounce scoops onto a baking sheet. Sprinkle tops with sugar. Bake approximately 20–25 minutes.

Serves 6.

—·—·—·—·—·—·—·—·—·—·—

Some people graduated to the rocker scoop and better pay. When my brother Elwood found work on the first commercial bogs, owned by Abel D. Makepeace, he faced an unofficial challenge from the more experienced workers. Elwood, a fierce competitor who was later known as "The Jim Thorpe of Cape Cod" because of his athleticism, finished the day twelve to fifteen boxes ahead of the next best worker, leaving the "regulars" shaking their heads.

The rocker scoop is built like the bottom of a rocking chair with wooden teeth. There are two varieties; one has parallel handles so that one hand is in front of the other. An ambidextrous person can switch from side to side. The other type has a single handle in the middle of the scoop. One hand pushes the scoop in and the other pulls it out, thus creating a rocking motion.

My father, Ferdinand "Smutt" Mills, taught Elwood and me. If fathers and grandfathers were good pickers, usually their sons, and in some cases, their daughters, would follow. This was strenuous work, primarily man's work, but there was one woman in particular I remember. Her name was Miss Octavia "Manthy" Avant. She was a big woman and a pretty good picker. She held her own pretty well; one of the few women I know who handled the rocker scoop. I'm sure there were others, but Miss Octavia sticks out in my mind.

CRANBERRY MINCEMEAT PIE

Pastry for 9-inch double crust
2 cups mincemeat

2 cups whole cranberry sauce
1 apple, peeled, cored and chopped

Preheat oven to 450°.

Line a pie plate with half of the pastry dough. Combine cranberry, mincemeat and apple. Turn into pie shell. Make a lattice top.

Bake for 10 minutes at 450°. Reduce heat to 350° and bake for an additional 25 minutes.

Serves 8.

CRANBERRY SQUARES

6 tablespoons butter
1 cup dark brown sugar, firmly
  packed
  OR add 1 tablespoon of molasses
  to a cup of light brown sugar
  OR add 2 tablespoons of
  molasses to a cup of white sugar
1 large egg

1 teaspoon vanilla
¾ cup all-purpose flour
½ teaspoon baking powder
¼ teaspoon salt
½–¾ cup nuts, chopped
¾ cup whole cranberries (fresh or
  fresh frozen), chopped coarsely

Preheat oven to 325°.

Grease an 8 x 8-inch inch baking pan. I prefer glass pans. Generously grease the pan, paying special attention to the corners. Line the bottom of the pan with a square of waxed paper and lightly butter the paper.

Place butter, sugar, egg and vanilla in a mixing bowl and beat at high speed for a minute or so until creamed. Combine flour, baking powder and salt in a separate bowl and mix thoroughly with a fork. Sprinkle over the butter mixture and slowly blend until all the flour is moistened (about a minute). **Do not overmix.**

Dust the cranberries with flour so they won't sink in the batter. Stir in the nuts and cranberries. Bake for 30-35 minutes.

Serves 6 to 8.

— . — . — . — . — . — . — . — . — . — . — . —

When it came time to get on the bogs, the kids and elders would hand pick by the six-quart measure on a fairly new bog that had just begun to produce. If we didn't have a measure, we'd bring pans or something to put the berries in and then we'd pour them into the measure and get a ticket for each measureful. Sometimes we'd get down on all fours for more speed. My father's words still echo in my ears, "Woosaung! Keep that scoop going!"

We could really gain some speed by twisting and pushing on that scoop instead of lifting it up and moving to another spot. When it was half to three-quarters full, we'd separate the vines and the berries, pull the vines out of the teeth and throw them back onto the bog. When the scoop got too heavy, we'd empty it into a box, making sure that the box was kept as close as possible. There was a lot of competition on the bog, so making the best use of time was almost as important as cutting down on the labor.

— . — . — . — . — . — . — . — . — . — . — . —

Six-quart measures for picked cranberries.

GOODIN' PUDDIN' AND GOODIN' PUDDIN' PIE

Goodin' Puddin' is a longtime favorite of ours. The recipe came from a dear friend, Ruth Ellis. Then Norman and Shirley Stolz, regular Flume patrons, gave us the recipe for cranberry pie, which is similar to Goodin' Puddin'. We've combined the two recipes into the following.

2 teaspoons cooking oil or butter	½ cup sugar
1 full cup cranberries	¼ cup melted butter
¾ cup sugar	1 egg
¼ cup nuts, coarsely chopped	½ cup flour

Preheat oven to 325°.

Grease an 8 x 4 x 4-inch loaf pan with the 2 teaspoons cooking oil or melted butter. Add the cranberries, ¼ cup sugar, and the nuts to loaf pan. Beat ½ cup sugar, ¼ cup melted butter and egg until smooth. Fold in flour and pour mixture over berries. Bake for 45 minutes.

You may double the recipe and bake in a deep-dish pie plate, for 6–8 servings.

Serves 4–6.

PEAR CRANBERRY CRISP

3 bosc pears, sliced
1 cup fresh cranberries
¼ cup maple syrup
2 teaspoons lemon juice
¼ cup brown sugar
½ cup oatmeal
  OR 1 cup fresh white bread,
  cubed

1 tablespoon butter
1 tablespoon flour
  OR 2 tablespoons butter and 1
  tablespoon cinnamon

Preheat oven to 400°.

Mix first four ingredients in a 1¼-quart (9 x 12-inch) baking dish. Mix and crumble sugar, oatmeal, butter and flour over the fruit.

Bake at 400° for 10 minutes. Reduce heat and bake at 350° for 25 minutes longer.

Serves 6.

— ▪ — ▪ — ▪ — ▪ — ▪ — ▪ — ▪ — ▪ — ▪ —

A tally keeper, usually the bog owner, assigned a number to each person. My father always had scoop #13. Elwood and I kept that number. When a box was full, we'd holler "#13." The tally keeper would repeat "13" and make a line on his clipboard for each of the first four boxes picked. The fifth time we called out our number, he'd draw a line through the others and call "tally 13." He'd repeat this for each succeeding five boxes.

We kept track of our numbers. Everyone had a pretty good idea how the others were doing. Every once in a while, the owner would come over and push his hand down into a bushel box of cranberries and discover that a picker had too many vines in his box. He'd take out all the vines and throw them onto the bog. "This looks like a rat's nest," he'd say. "Better put a few more berries into the box."

— ▪ — ▪ — ▪ — ▪ — ▪ — ▪ — ▪ — ▪ — ▪ —

Rocker scoop.

DESSERTS

HAPPY ENDINGS

The end of a meal signals a forthcoming treat. Our desserts are selections reminiscent of bygone days as well as current favorites. There's a certain comfort in returning to the kitchens of our youth and rediscovering our roots.

We've tested recipes and traversed cranberry bogs; visited Corn Hill, Hobomock's Village at Plimoth Plantation and The Mashantucket Pequot Museum and Research Center, and retested recipes. In so doing, we walked familiar paths and Betty experienced history. I have suggested that the reason she fell into the marginal ditch on a very soggy bog is that she's a descendent of those pious thieves who raided the Indians' corn so long ago on Corn Hill.

Our cookbook isn't just another pretty cover. It's the blending of the two cultures who met at that first Thanksgiving. We'd like you to share in this Common Table.

It's important that we end on a sweet note. This has been a labor of love. Both Betty and I have met interesting and thoughtful people, eaten well and had a great time with this book. We hope you will, too!

Picket fence.

Wildflowers strewn along grassy hillside near beach at Cape Cod.

We wish to give a greeting and thanksgiving
To the Spirits of the People
That have combined to carry forth
The beliefs and protection of our People.
We recognize that the Great Mystery
Has provided that Spirit,
And that it is part of our instructions
To combine our spirits for the good of all Life.

— from The Longest Walk Manifesto

APPLE BROWN BETTY

Good cooking apples are imperative for the success of this dish! The Apple Brown Betty pan should be set over a larger baking pan to catch the juices that may boil over.

3 pounds (5–6 cups) cooking
  apples
1 tablespoon water
1 teaspoon white sugar
12 tablespoons (1½ sticks) melted
  butter or margarine

5 teaspoons cinnamon
¾ cup light brown sugar, firmly
  packed
10 slices fresh white bread with
  crust, cut into ½-inch cubes

Preheat oven to 375°.

Peel, core and slice apples into a saucepan. Add water and sugar. Cover. Simmer to soften apples.

Pour 3 tablespoons of the melted butter, 1½ teaspoons of the cinnamon and ⅛ cup of the brown sugar into the bottom of a baking pan. With the back of a spoon, mix the ingredients thoroughly.

Cover the bottom of the pan with about ⅓ of the bread, followed by ½ of the apples, evenly layered with some of the juice from the cooked apples. Add a layer of the bread with another 1½ teaspoons of the cinnamon sprinkled over the bread, another ⅛ cup of the brown sugar crumbled over the bread and another 3 tablespoons of the melted butter drizzled over the bread mixture. Add the remaining half of the apples and juice evenly layered over the bread.

Finish by topping with the remaining bread, 2 tablespoons of cinnamon and ½ cup of brown sugar. Drizzle the last 6 tablespoons of butter over all. Cover tightly with foil and bake for 55 minutes, carefully removing the foil for the last 10–15 minutes of baking to brown and crisp the bread.

Serve with whipped cream or ice cream.

Serves 6–8.

BAKED PEACHES
(from former First Lady Barbara Bush, Walker's Point, Maine)

We were pleased to receive this recipe from the former First Lady along with the following note:

> Thanks so much for your nice letter requesting a recipe with a fond remembrance. I am forwarding a copy of my recipe for Baked Peaches, which is often served at Walker's Point. It is an easy recipe, but it is always met with rave reviews and, best of all, it reminds me of the times our family is together in Maine.
>
> This is our son Jeb's favorite dessert, and we have it on his first night here always.
>
> With all best wishes,
>
> Warmly,
> Barbara Bush

Del Monte peach halves in heavy syrup, ½ peach per serving
butter
brown sugar
cinnamon
lemon juice
real whipped cream
optional: rum

Preheat oven to 350°.

Place peach halves in flat baking dish with half of their syrup.

Place a "dab" of butter and a "dab" of brown sugar in the center of each peach. Sprinkle with cinnamon and squeeze lemon juice over.

Bake until brown and until some of the juice melts away. If you wish, you may cover with rum, light and serve. Pass a bowl of real whipped cream.

½ peach per serving.

BREAD PUDDING

All ingredients go into the top part of a double boiler over boiling water. The secret of this pudding is in the double boiler. I prefer to concoct my own, using a four-quart pan to hold the water and a two-quart stainless steel bowl or pan to hold the pudding.

1 cup brown sugar, packed
3–5 slices bread, well buttered*
3 eggs
2 cups milk
¼ teaspoon salt

1 teaspoon vanilla
2 teaspoons nutmeg
optional: ¼ cup raisins
   I like thick unsliced bread, such as Portuguese, Italian or French bread that will sit in the bottom of the pan.

Remove most of the crust as the crust doesn't soften. Cut the bread into slices that are 1½–2 inches thick. Butter one side of each thoroughly. Set aside.

Place ½ cup of the brown sugar in the top of the double boiler and spread evenly, sides and all. Add half of the raisins, if using, to the top of the brown sugar and spread evenly. Add half of the bread, buttered sides down. Beat the eggs. Add milk, salt and vanilla to the eggs. Do not stir. Pour half of the egg/milk mixture over bread. Add the balance of the brown sugar, then layer with the remaining raisins, bread and egg/milk mixture. Sprinkle with nutmeg. Bring to a low simmer, cover, and steam for one hour over a low flame. Let stand for another ½ hour and invert into a serving dish, spreading the brown sugar around the pudding.

Serve with whipped cream.

Serves 6–8.

CHEESECAKE
(from Trish Gavel)

1 pound cream cheese*
3 eggs
2/3 cup sugar
1/2 teaspoon almond extract

Topping
1 cup sour cream*
3 tablespoons sugar
1 teaspoon vanilla
Crushed berries

If substituting non-fat cream cheese and/or light sour cream for these ingredients, the cake will be slightly less firm to cut.

**Frozen berries are best because they have more liquid.*

Preheat oven to 350°. Grease a 9-inch pie plate.

Beat cream cheese, eggs and sugar thoroughly. Add almond extract. Pour into pie plate. Bake for 25 minutes. Cool for 20 minutes.

While cake is cooling, make topping. Beat sour cream, sugar, vanilla and berries together. Pour this mixture over the top of the cheesecake. Return to 350° oven and bake 10 minutes longer.

Serves 8.

CRANBERRY DESSERTS

For desserts made with carnberries, *see* recipes on pp.153, 155 and 156.

DOUGHNUTS

3½ cups all-purpose flour (plus
    extra for dusting rolling pin and
    work surface)
1 cup sugar
½ teaspoon baking soda
2 teaspoons baking powder
1 teaspoon salt
½ teaspoon ground nutmeg

¾ cup buttermilk,
    OR add 1 tablespoon of white
    vinegar to 1 cup of milk
4 tablespoons butter, melted
2 eggs
1 egg yolk
optional: Powdered sugar or
    cinnamon sugar for dusting

Combine 1 cup of the flour with the other dry ingredients in the bowl of a mixer.

In another bowl, whisk together the buttermilk, butter, eggs and yolk. Pour the liquids into the dry ingredients and beat for 10–12 seconds. Lower speed and add remaining 2½ cups of flour and mix until just combined, about 30 seconds. Stir up the dough to make sure that all of the liquid is absorbed.

Heat oil to 375° in a large Dutch oven or electric fryer. Test with a candy thermometer. While oil is heating, dust the work surface and rolling pin liberally with flour. Roll out the dough to ½-inch thickness. Cut each doughnut with a well-floured doughnut cutter. Flour cutter after each cutting. Let the doughnuts sit for five minutes. Gather scraps and roll them out again.

When oil reaches 375°, fry several doughnuts (depends on size of pan). When doughnuts rise to the top, flip and cook for approximately 50 seconds. Remove holes and test for doneness. Remove to absorbent paper with a slotted spoon. Dust with powdered sugar or cinnamon sugar, if desired, and enjoy.

Place in a cool place in a tightly covered canister. Because doughnuts taste best when warm, reheat in oven for serving.

Serves 8–10.

EMMA OAKLEY MILLS' HOT MILK CAKE

2 eggs
1 cup sugar
1 cup sifted flour
1 teaspoon baking powder
¼ teaspoon salt

½ cup milk
1 tablespoon butter
1 teaspoon flavoring (vanilla, lemon, etc.)

Preheat oven to 375°. Grease and flour 8 x 8-inch pan.

Beat eggs well. Gradually add sugar and beat until very light. Combine and add flour, baking powder and salt. Place milk and butter in sauce pan. Heat just to boiling and add to previous mixture. Add flavoring and mix well.

Bake for 35 minutes.

Serves 6.

EMMA OAKLEY MILLS' MAYO CAKE

2 cups flour
1 cup sugar
4 tablespoons cocoa
1½ teaspoons baking soda
1 cup mayonnaise
1 cup water
1 teaspoon vanilla

Frosting
1 cup sugar
½ cup white corn syrup
¼ cup cold water
¾ teaspoon cream of tartar
½ cup egg whites

Preheat oven to 350°.

Sift together flour, sugar, cocoa and baking soda. Then add mayonnaise, water and vanilla. Bake 20-25 minutes.

For frosting, combine sugar, corn syrup, and water over low heat, stirring often. Boil to 238° on a candy thermometer, or until syrup spins a thread.

Beat egg whites with cream of tartar until stiff and add "boiled" ingredients slowly while beating. Beat until frosting peaks and holds its shape.

Serves 8.

GINGERBREAD COOKIES
(from Massachusetts Congressman William Delahunt)

This a rich, delicious cookie that keeps its crispiness best in a cookie tin.

½ cup shortening
½ cup sugar
½ cup boiling water
¾ cup molasses
2¼ cups flour

1 teaspoon ginger
1 teaspoon cinnamon
1 teaspoon baking powder
1½ teaspoons baking soda
sugar for topping

Preheat oven to 350°.

Beat shortening for about one minute. Add sugar. Beat until fluffy. Heat water to boiling and add molasses, dissolving the molasses. Set aside.

Sift the dry ingredients. Add to the beaten sugar and shortening. Add in molasses and water mixture. Mix well. Spoon onto a cookie sheet, leaving room for each cookie to bake.

Bake for 11 minutes in preheated oven. When cookies are done, sprinkle just a bit of sugar on them.

The same recipe makes a wonderful gingerbread. Bake in a greased 8 x 8-inch pan for 35–40 minutes.

GRAPE NUT PUDDING

1 cup sugar	2 teaspoons butter, melted
4 eggs, beaten	1½ teaspoons vanilla
3 cups milk	¾ cup grape nuts
1 cup heavy cream	1½ teaspoon nutmeg

Preheat oven to 350°. Grease a 9 x 9-inch baking pan or two 8 x 4-inch loaf pans.

Cream the sugar and eggs. Add all of the remaining ingredients except the grape nuts and nutmeg. Pour into buttered casserole, or baking pans. Pour grape nuts evenly over the mixture.

Set baking dishes or casserole in a pan of water. Bake for 1 hour. Stir twice during first ½ hour of baking to blend so grape nuts won't sink to the bottom of the pan.

Remove from oven and sprinkle the nutmeg on top.

Serves 6–8.

Earl with son Robert Mills at Mashpee Pow Wow.

STRAWBERRY COBBLER

1 quart strawberries
½ cup sugar

1½ teaspoons lemon juice
1 tablespoon corn starch

Coarsely crush berries with a potato masher.
   Add the sugar to the berries and bring to a boil for five minutes.
Combine the lemon juice and corn starch and add to the berry mixture.
   Serve over Baking Powder Biscuits (*see* recipe below).

Serves 6.

BAKING POWDER BISCUITS
for Strawberry Cobbler

2 cups flour, sifted
2½ teaspoons baking powder
1 teaspoon salt

¼ cup shortening
¾ cup milk

Preheat oven to 450°. Combine dry ingredients in large mixing bowl. Cut
in shortening until mixture is the consistency of corn meal. Stir in most
of the milk, adding the remainder of the milk until the dough is pliable.
Too much milk will produce a sticky dough; too little will make the biscuits dry. Round up the dough on a lightly floured board. Knead about
six times, being careful not too handle the dough too much. Roll the
dough out to ¼-inch thickness. Using a cookie cutter or the mouth of a
jar or drinking glass, cut out biscuits in close circles. Remaining dough
may be rolled out (not kneaded) and formed into additional circles.
   Place the dough circles close together on an ungreased cookie sheet. If
the baking sheet has sides, invert it and bake the biscuits on the flat bottom. Bake on the middle rack of the oven until golden brown, about
10–12 minutes.

Makes approximately 20 biscuits.

INDIAN PUDDING

One recipe caused a heated "discussion" between Betty and me. In deference to my dear sister Delscena, I simply couldn't part with her recipe for Indian Pudding. However, Betty insisted that if I didn't put The Flume's own Indian Pudding in this book, I couldn't substitute another. After much deliberation and prodding, we came up with a delectable replacement, nearly identical in flavor and memories, without divulging Delscena's secret ingredient.

4 cups milk
⅓ cup corn meal
¾ cup molasses
2 eggs

1 teaspoon salt
8 ginger snaps
¼ teaspoon ginger

Combine all of the ingredients in a double boiler and whip over simmering water.

Continue to cook over a low flame for an additional 1–1½ hours, whipping occasionally, until pudding starts to thicken. Once it starts to thicken, remove the whip and allow the pudding to thicken naturally and form a skim or crust on top.

Serve warm with vanilla ice cream or whipped cream.

If serving later, refrigerate. Warm in a microwave or double boiler. Add milk, if necessary.

Serves 6 to 8.

HINTS AND SUGGESTIONS

Measurements

We discovered that many measuring spoons and cups are not standardized; the amounts vary from brand to brand. The following methods of measuring should help you gauge the correct amounts. One method is applicable to shortening and liquid; the other for any standard measurement.

Butter

¼ pound	=	8 tablespoons
2 tablespoons	=	1 ounce
4 tablespoons	=	¼ cup
3 teaspoons	=	1 tablespoon
1½ teaspoons	=	1 ounce

Liquid

2 tablespoons	=	1 ounce
¼ cup	=	2 ounces
3 tablespoons	=	¼ cup
3 teaspoons	=	1 tablespoon
8 ounces	=	1 cup

Standard Equivalents

3 teaspoons	=	1 tablespoon
1 tablespoon	=	3 teaspoons
4 tablespoons	=	¼ cup
5⅓ tablespoons	=	⅓ cup
8 tablespoons	=	½ cup
12 tablespoons	=	¾ cup
16 tablespoons	=	1 cup
1 cup	=	½ pint
4 cups	=	1 quart
16 ounces	=	1 pound
32 ounces	=	1 quart

Suggestions

Brown sugar: To keep brown sugar from hardening, add an apple to an air-tight jar. If you don't have any brown sugar on hand, add one tablespoon of molasses to one cup of white sugar.

Buttermilk or soured milk: Add one tablespoon of white vinegar to one cup of milk.

Butter: To prevent butter from burning when heating, replace a little of the butter with oil or use half oil and half butter.

To clarify butter, cut butter into small pieces. Melt over low heat. Don't let the edges brown. Let cool for a few minutes. Spoon the clear yellow liquid on top into a small bowl. Discard the frothy white residue on the bottom or save to use in cooking.

For seasoned butter (for fish or meat), start with soft butter and work strong ingredients, like anchovies or bone marrow, into the butter and shape it into a thin log for easy slicing.

For maitre d'hotel butter (for fish), add one tablespoon chopped fresh parsley, salt, pepper and one teaspoon lemon rind to one tablespoon butter and smooth out the butter. Wrap in a piece of plastic wrap and shape it into a roll. Refrigerate before cutting. Place one slice on each piece of fish as soon as it comes out of the oven.

Roux: To make a roux, combine shortening and flour or corn meal and cook to the consistency of corn meal. Cooking utilizes the total thickening power of the flour. When blended to the proper consistency, there is no floury taste. The thickening agent can also be made with arrowroot or cornstarch mixed with water or stock; especially when a clear, glossy sauce is preferred, such as in jardiniere sauce.

Taste: When cooking, we must taste as we go along. Testing for the right amount of seasoning is the essence of good cooking.

Salt: Salt is a flavor enhancer. Be careful that it doesn't take over. It should just provide a delicate balance.

GLOSSARY

base—a concentrated meat paste or granule used to enhance and bring out flavors in dishes

black spider—cast iron frying pan, which originally had legs on it for use on a hearth or wood burning stove, consequently the name "spider"

blanch—to drop into hot water or oil to soften, to scald

bog—wet spongy ground, a small marsh, used for growing cranberries

braise—to brown in fat

bull rake—tool used for scalloping

Bundt pan—a decorative cake pan with scalloped sides

calumet—ceremonial Native American pipe

Chinese cut—a method of slicing at an angle, rotating the item as you slice so that the slices are cut on a diagonal and are not symmetrical in size or shape. The variety of the slices adds to the esthetics and texture of the dish.

cornstarch—a fine granular or powdery starch made from corn

crane-berries—name given to cranberries by Pilgrims

creel—a basket with a hole in the top that is carried over the shoulder and used for carrying freshly caught fish

dry harvesting—harvesting cranberries by hand or scoop picking on dry bogs

eel spear—a long, narrow, flexible spear with prongs for spearing eels

finnan haddie—smoked cod or haddock

The Flume—Earl Mills' restaurant in Mashpee, Massachusetts, on Cape Cod. Named after an edifice for storing or controlling water.

garni (bouquet garni)—a garnish, usually a combination of parsley, thyme and bay leaves, which is tied in a cheesecloth bag for easy removal

gelatin—of the consistency of jelly

hand reel—tool for separating cranberries from vines; looks like a scoop on a lawn mower

head cheese—not cheese at all, rather a loaf of jellied, seasoned meat derived from a pig's head

hominy—meal made from parched corn

julienne—to cut into thin strips

Kiehtan—the Principal Maker of All

Kietannit—the spirit of Kiehtan

linguica—a Portuguese sausage

maize—corn

Mannits—gods

marginal ditch—ditch around the perimeter of the bog to keep the "good" on and the "bad" off

mashpee—big water or big cove

measure—6-quart wooden or tin bucket for measuring picked cranberries

medicine man—*Pau Wau*, the spiritual leader of a tribe

milt—the dark, oily part of an oily fish

mussel—a dark-colored shellfish.

parboil—to boil briefly as a preliminary or incomplete cooking procedure

pâté—a spread of finely mashed seasoned and spiced meat

poke (pokeweed)—a weed with a tobacco-like leaf that grows on a hollow, wet bush in the woodlands

pone—a small loaf of corn bread

Pow Wow—from *Pau Wau*, meaning medicine man. Originally, a Pow Wow was a trip to the medicine, a meeting of tribal leaders who would discuss problems. Today, a Pow Wow is a social and commercial venture that brings together many different tribes from across the nation. Dance, music and food are integral parts of the event; dance and drumming competitions have led to changes in traditions and dress as participants borrow steps and art from other groups.

quahog—any hard-shell clam. Varying names relate to the size. Littlenecks are the smallest, followed in size by cherrystones, necks and chowder 'hogs.

reduce—to cook down in order to make richer

reels ("eggbeaters")—flat-tired vehicles used in wet harvesting to separate the cranberries from the vines

render—to melt down, as fat

rocker scoop—scoop with teeth and parallel handles and a base shaped like the bottom of a rocking chair, used in picking cranberries

rockweed—a seaweed used in clambakes that grows in the crevices of rocks. Sacs in the brownish-green weed hold saltwater, which provides the food with a salty flavor and steam.

roe—fish eggs

roux—a cooked mixture of butter or other fat and flour. Used to thicken sauces, soups and gravies.

Sachem—a leader of a tribe who is responsible for his people's welfare and government.

salmi sauce—sauce used to marinate and tenderize wild duck or goose and reduce its gaminess while cooking

Sassamenesh—Algonkian word for cranberry

sauté—to fry quickly with a little fat

scald—to heat almost to the boiling point

scalloper—one who fishes for scallops

scallop glass—box with glass on the bottom, used in looking for scallops

shad—a fish

snap scoop—one-hand scoop with metal teeth, that opens and closes with a snapping sound and encloses cranberies then pulls them off the vines

split—small bottle of champagne, enough for two servings

stock—water in which meat, fish or vegetables had been cooked. Used as a base for soups and sauces.

tally—count of picked cranberries

Three Sisters—corn, squash and beans

Turtle Island—Native American name for Earth

U-10—a number that denotes the size of a shrimp. U-10 means that there are ten or less shrimp to a pound; these, of course, would be larger than U-12s or U-24s (12 or less or 24 or less to a pound).

vinaigrette—a salad dressing or cold sauce made of vinegar, herbs, oil, etc.

washboiler—large, 8–10 gallon, covered pot, like an old washtub

Weetabix—brand name of a cereal similar to Shredded Wheat

wet harvesting—flooding the cranberry bogs before harvesting, using heavy machinery

wheeler—a worker who went into the bogs to remove the day's harvest with an extended wheelbarrow

whisk—a wire beater

ALGONKIAN GLOSSARY

The Wampanoag language is derived from the Algonkian tongue of the Algonquian people. Translations are complicated since words are complex, made up of a myriad of prefixes and suffixes. Many words have several meanings; all are descriptive of places and people. The following words are loosely-translated and intended to help the reader understand our narratives.

appanaug—clambake

askutasquash—squash

Esquagannit—Spirit of the Woman

ho—Amen. So be it.

k—goes on now, still continuing

Kesuckquandannit—Spirit of the Sun

Kesuck—The Heavens

Kiehtan—Principal Maker of All. Great God. Antiquity.

Koh-mus-so-quam-k-an-nit—Cape Cod (mussoquam—a ripe ear of corn; k—goes on now, still continuing; annit—spirit) Spirit of the Land that allows the corn to grow

Manitoo—"God is."

Munnannock (Monadnock)—A place where one can see the sun and the moon

Musquantum—The Devil

mussoquam—a ripe ear of corn

Nanapaushat—Spirit of the Moon

Nipmuck—fresh water place

Noohkik—a mixture of ground parched or roasted corn, which early native people carried in pouches tied around their waists. When they were out on hunting or fishing expeditions, they added water, honey or juice from wild berries and made little cakes that provided them sustenance on their journey. Also called a Johnny cake.

Ohkeannit—Spirit of Mother Earth

Paupangausit—Spirit of the Ocean

petukquineg—bread

pumukan—dance

Sachem—a leader of a tribe who is responsible for his people's welfare and government.

sikkissuog—a soft-shell clam

sobaheg—soup, stew

Suckamore—A lesser chief, small sachem. Used to describe a small bird that follows a larger one. Also the origin of the word Sagamore, as in the Sagamore Bridge.

tavern—a pile of sticks thrown by passersby asking protection on their journies

tuppuhquamash—beans

Wabanannit—Spirit of the Wind

wampa—prefix meaning light, whiteness, the east

Wampanoag—People of the Early Light, of the East

Wampanannit—Spirit of the Light

wampi—white, or light

wetu—house

Wetuannit—Spirit of the House

weyaus—meat

Wutchekan—It yields produce. Seacoast people gave this name to the ocean as "the great producer" of fishes, their staple food.

Wutchekannit—The Great Producer

Yotannit—Spirit of Fire

INDEX

blackberries, 105
blanch, 114, 173
blinds, hunting, 70
blueberries, xi, 105
bluefish, 74
boat(s), xi, 35, 72
bog(s), cranberry, xi, 139, 143–145, 173
  bog owner(s), 145, 157
bok choy, 30
Boneless Roast of Veal, 49
Boston Marathon, 84
Boston, Massachusetts, 13
bows, 105
Bradford, William, 125
brandy, 41
Bread Pudding, 163
Breaded Scallops, 102
breads, 13–21, 156, 161, 163
  Apple Chunk Bread, 17
  Baking Powder Biscuits, 169
  Banana Nut Bread, 18
  Bean Pot Bread, 13
  Cape Cod Cranberry Scones, 151
  Cranberry Coffee Cake, 149
  Cranberry Nut Bread, 150
  Emma Oakley Mills' Fry Bread, 15
  Indian Fry Bread, 14
  Irish Soda Bread, 19
  Lemon Bread, 20
  Morning Bread, 15
  Pie Crust, 16
  Senator John F. Kerry's Cranberry Bread, 148
  Zucchini Bread, 20
  See also corn breads.
Breen, Betty, xiv, 42, 84, 122, 159, 190
Britain, 127
broccoli, 8, 25, 30, 65, 114
Broiled Salmon, 76
Broiled Tomato, 121
broth, 97
  broth, chicken, 137
Brown, Jim "Choctaw," 55
Bryant, Solomon, 145
Bryant's Neck, 145

bull rake, 140, 173
Bundt pan, 173
Bush, Barbara, 133, 162
Bush, George, 133
Bussey Institute, 124
butter, 171, 172
  butter, clarified, 172
  butter, maitre d'hotel, 172
  butter, seasoned, 172
buttermilk, 165, 172
Butternut Squash, 121
cabbage, 10, 22, 51
  Cabbage, 117
Caesar Salad, 21
calumet, 173
calumet, or pipe, dance, 110
candy thermometer, 166
Cape Cod Canal, 84, 95
Cape Cod Cranberry Scones, 151
Cape Cod League, 105
Cape Cod, Massachusetts, xii, xiii, 10, 13, 23, 71, 84, 113, 125, 139, 143, 151, 160
capers, 9
carrots, 9, 30, 33, 43, 44, 45, 50, 51, 54, 57, 58, 59, 67, 70
  Carrots, 118
  glazed, 118
  nutmeg, 118
  parslied, 118
Carter, Bernard, 33
Carver, Massachusetts, 145
Catholic Stew, 55
cauliflower, 114
celery, 9, 11, 12, 27, 43, 44, 45, 50, 54, 55, 58, 59, 61, 62, 63, 65, 66, 98, 99, 103, 137
champagne, 49
Champagne Sauce, 49
cheddar cheese, 134
cheese, 31, 133
  cheddar, 134
  cream, 164
  parmesan, 24, 114, 121
cheesecake, 164
cheesecloth, 92, 96

MEET THE AUTHORS

Earl Mills Sr.

At a time when so many are seeking their roots, **Earl Mills'** every footstep falls on his ancestors' path. Educator, athlete, restaurateur, author, and public speaker, Mills' primary passion is preserving his heritage. He is the chief, or sachem, of the Mashpee Wampanoags and has been the owner of his Cape Cod restaurant, The Flume, for over 27 years.

When Mills was named chief of the Mashpee Wampanoags, he adopted the Indian name of *Wampsikuk,* or Chief Flying Eagle. As chief of his people, he has been an advocate for their rights and the preservation of their heritage through the annual Pow Wow as well as public speaking engagements and writings for various publications. Currently involved with the Mashpee Archives and the Mashpee Historical Society, he is also serving as president of the Old Indian Meeting House in Mashpee.

Mills is also the author of *Son of Mashpee,* a compilation of short stories about his people, his childhood recollections and tales from his elders.

Betty Breen

Betty Breen is a freelance writer who lives with her husband Bob in Westwood and North Falmouth, Massachusetts. Before and after raising her family, she pursued various occupations—medical assistant, real estate broker and appraiser, insurance broker, and antique shop proprietor, all the while being an avid cook.

In the fall of 1997, while enrolled in a graduate writing program at Harvard, Breen was assigned a research paper that resulted in her search for native people to interview. Four telephone calls to friends on Cape Cod resulted in one name. Within months of interviewing Earl Mills, she had accepted his offer to write his cookbook.

In the process of creating this book, Breen has avidly adopted Mills' respect for the land. She has discovered the miracle of the ongoing cycle of life through the seasons, the native traditions and values, the herring runs and the cranberry bogs. She is currently editing her first novel, *Soft Shoulders,* as well as a children's book.